CW01150721

Preface to "Inflation-Proof Cookbook: Meals Under $3" by Chef Joe Ciminera

As I stand in my kitchen, surrounded by the comforting aroma of simmering ingredients, I find myself reflecting on the journey that has brought me to this moment. My career as a chef has been a remarkable adventure—one that has taken me from the bustling kitchens of Michelin-starred restaurants to hosting exclusive tasting events where guests indulge in culinary creations priced at $1,000 per plate. These experiences have shaped my culinary philosophy and deepened my love for food, but they have also opened my eyes to a pressing issue that many families face today: the staggering rise in food costs that makes it increasingly difficult to afford nutritious meals.

In recent years, we have witnessed a significant transformation in the landscape of food pricing. The confluence of inflation, supply chain challenges, and global events has created a perfect storm that has driven food prices to alarming levels. Families are feeling the impact in their wallets, and what was once a straightforward grocery trip has turned into a daunting task. I have spoken with countless friends, family members, and community members who express their frustrations over the rising cost of groceries and the difficulty of providing healthy meals for their loved ones. As a father who cooks for my family every night, I understand firsthand the emotional toll that comes with trying to balance a budget while ensuring that my family enjoys wholesome, satisfying meals.

It was this realization that inspired me to write "Inflation-Proof Cookbook: Meals Under $3." This book is my heartfelt response to the challenges many families are grappling with in today's economic climate. My mission is to demonstrate that cooking can still be a joyful, fulfilling experience, even when faced with tight budgets. I want to show you that it's possible to create delicious meals without breaking the bank, proving that high-quality, flavorful food doesn't have to come with a hefty price tag.

In "Inflation-Proof Cookbook," you will find an extensive collection of recipes designed to cost no more than $3 per serving. Each dish reflects my culinary philosophy that affordability and flavor can coexist beautifully. From hearty soups and comforting casseroles to vibrant salads and flavorful pasta dishes, this cookbook offers a diverse array of options that cater to a variety of tastes and dietary preferences. I want to take you on a culinary journey that proves delicious, nutritious meals can be accessible to everyone, regardless of their financial situation.

But this book goes beyond just providing recipes; it serves as a comprehensive guide to navigating the complexities of cooking on a budget. I believe that with the right strategies and a bit of creativity, anyone can become a smart shopper. Throughout these pages, you will discover practical tips on how to shop effectively, including meal planning, bulk buying, and selecting seasonal ingredients that offer the best value. By focusing on these strategies, you will not only stretch your grocery dollars but also reduce food waste, making the most of every ingredient.

Meal planning is a game changer. By dedicating a little time each week to outline your meals, you can create a focused shopping list that minimizes impulse buys and keeps you on track. I encourage you to think about how to incorporate ingredients you already have in your pantry into your meal plans. This not only helps you save money but also inspires creativity in the kitchen. Cooking should be an adventure, not a chore. Embrace the challenge of turning ordinary ingredients into extraordinary dishes.

Moreover, "Inflation-Proof Cookbook" emphasizes the importance of resourcefulness in the kitchen. In an era where prices seem to climb daily, we must harness our creativity and adaptability. I want to encourage you to view cooking as an opportunity for innovation. Don't be afraid to experiment with recipes, swap out ingredients, or make adjustments based on what you have on hand. This flexibility will not only save you money but will also empower you to take ownership of your cooking journey. Each meal can become a canvas for your culinary creativity, and I am excited to see what you will create.

The recipes in this book are designed to be straightforward and approachable, with step-by-step instructions that make them easy to replicate. I understand that cooking for a family can feel overwhelming, especially with busy schedules and competing priorities. That's why I've crafted these recipes to be not only affordable but also quick and satisfying. I want you to find joy in the cooking process, reclaiming the sense of accomplishment that comes from preparing a delicious meal for those you love.

Additionally, cooking is about more than just the food—it's about the connections we forge around the table. I encourage you to involve your family in the cooking process, inviting your children, partners, or friends to join you. Cooking together fosters teamwork, strengthens relationships, and creates cherished memories. It's in these moments that we build lasting bonds, sharing laughter, stories, and love over the meals we prepare. I hope you find joy in this communal experience, knowing that you are not just nourishing your bodies but also enriching your lives.

As we navigate the complexities of rising food costs, "Inflation-Proof Cookbook" serves as a beacon of hope. It's a reminder that even in challenging times, we can find ways to enjoy the simple pleasures of cooking and eating together. This book is a testament to the resilience of families everywhere who refuse to let economic pressures dictate their culinary experiences. Together, we can redefine the narrative around affordable food, proving that it can be delicious, satisfying, and deeply fulfilling.

In closing, I want to extend my heartfelt gratitude to you for allowing me into your kitchen. Thank you for embracing this journey with me as we explore the beauty of affordable meals and the joy of gathering around the table. "Inflation-Proof Cookbook: Meals Under $3" is not just a collection of recipes; it is a celebration of resilience, creativity, and the power of home-cooked meals to bring us together. Let's embark on this culinary adventure, turning the challenge of rising food costs into an opportunity for exploration, connection, and joy. With a little creativity, resourcefulness, and love, we can create something truly special—one affordable meal at a time. God Bless you and your family!

Chef Joe Ciminera

Acknowledgments

Writing "Inflation-Proof Cookbook: Meals Under $3" has been a labor of love, and I am deeply grateful to everyone who has supported me throughout this journey.

First and foremost, I want to thank my family, who are my toughest critics at the dinner table every night. Your honest feedback and discerning palates have pushed me to elevate my cooking and create meals that satisfy both taste and budget. It's your expectations that motivate me to ensure every recipe is not only delicious but also worthy of our shared table.

I would also like to acknowledge my mentors and culinary colleagues who have guided me along my culinary path. Your wisdom and insights have profoundly shaped my understanding of food and its power to bring people together. From the bustling kitchens of fine dining to the warmth of home cooking, your influence is reflected in every recipe within these pages.

A heartfelt thank you goes out to my loyal followers on TikTok and my fans from my cooking show series on PBS, Taste This TV. Your continued support and enthusiasm inspire me every day. You motivate me to share my passion for cooking, and I am grateful for the vibrant community we've built together. Your comments, shares, and love for food have fueled my creativity and passion for this craft.

To the countless families who shared their stories and challenges with me, thank you for opening up and allowing me to understand your struggles in today's challenging economic climate. Your voices have inspired me to create a cookbook that truly resonates with those seeking to nourish their families without breaking the bank.

I am grateful to the talented photographers, editors, and designers who worked tirelessly to bring this book to life. Your creativity and dedication have transformed my vision into a beautifully presented collection of recipes, making it accessible and appealing to all.

Lastly, I want to thank you, the reader. Your willingness to embark on this culinary adventure with me means the world. I hope that this cookbook not only provides you with delicious, budget-friendly meals but also inspires you to explore your creativity in the kitchen. Together, let's embrace the joy of cooking, making memorable meals for ourselves and our loved ones.

With gratitude and love,

Chef Joe Ciminera

Eggplant and Tomato Salad

Ingredients:

- 1 medium eggplant ($1.00)
- 1 large tomato ($0.75)
- 1 tablespoon olive oil ($0.25)
- Salt and pepper to taste ($0.05)
- A sprinkle of dried oregano ($0.10)

Instructions:

1. Dice the eggplant and roast it with olive oil for about 20 minutes until tender.
2. Dice the tomato and mix it with the roasted eggplant.
3. Add salt, pepper, and oregano to taste.

Cost per serving: ~$2.15 (serves 4)

Pepper and Cucumber Salad

Ingredients:

- 1 large bell pepper ($0.75)
- 1 cucumber ($0.75)
- 2 tablespoons vinegar ($0.10)
- 1 tablespoon olive oil ($0.25)
- Salt and pepper to taste ($0.05)

Instructions:

1. Thinly slice the bell pepper and cucumber.
2. Toss them with vinegar, olive oil, salt, and pepper.

Cost per serving: ~$1.90 (serves 3)

Carrot and Cabbage Slaw

Ingredients:

- 1/4 head of cabbage ($0.50)
- 2 medium carrots ($0.50)
- 2 tablespoons mayonnaise ($0.25)
- 1 tablespoon vinegar ($0.10)
- Salt and pepper to taste ($0.05)

Instructions:

1. 1Shred the cabbage and carrots.
2. 2Mix them with mayonnaise, vinegar, salt, and pepper.

Cost per serving: ~$1.40 (serves 4)

Lettuce and Chickpea Salad

Ingredients:

- 1 head of lettuce ($1.00)
- 1/2 can chickpeas, drained ($0.75)
- 2 tablespoons lemon juice ($0.10)
- 1 tablespoon olive oil ($0.25)
- Salt and pepper to taste ($0.05)

Instructions:

1. Tear the lettuce and mix it with chickpeas.
2. Toss with lemon juice, olive oil, salt, and pepper.

Cost per serving: ~$2.15 (serves 3)

Pasta Salad with Bell Peppers

Ingredients:

- 1 cup cooked pasta ($0.50)
- 1 bell pepper, diced ($0.75)
- 1 tablespoon olive oil ($0.25)
- 1 tablespoon vinegar ($0.10)
- Salt and pepper to taste ($0.05)
- 2 Tablespoon mayonnaise ($0.60)
- Black pepper for ($0.10)

Instructions:

1. Cook the pasta and let it cool.
2. Mix with diced bell pepper, olive oil, vinegar, salt, and pepper.

Cost per serving: ~$2.35 (serves 2)

Deviled Eggs

Ingredients:

- 6 large eggs ($1.00)
- 2 tablespoons mayonnaise ($0.10)
- 1 teaspoon mustard ($0.05)
- Salt, pepper, and paprika for seasoning ($0.05)

Instructions:

1. Hard boil the eggs and let them cool.
2. Cut eggs in half, remove yolks, and mix them with mayonnaise, mustard, salt, and pepper.
3. Pipe or spoon the yolk mixture back into the egg whites, and sprinkle with paprika.

Cost: $1.20 for about 12 halves.

Cucumber Bites with Cream Cheese

Ingredients:

- 1 cucumber ($0.80)
- 4 oz cream cheese ($1.20)
- 1 teaspoon dill or seasoning ($0.05)
- Small capers ($0.50)

Instructions:

1. Slice cucumber into rounds.
2. Spread cream cheese on each slice and sprinkle with dill.

Cost: $2.55 for 20-25 pieces.

Garlic Toast

Ingredients:

- 1 loaf of French bread ($1.00)
- 2 tablespoons butter ($0.20)
- 2 cloves garlic, minced ($0.10)
- Parsley for garnish (optional) ($0.05)
- 1 ounce of mozzarella cheese ($1.00)

Instructions:

1. Slice the bread and toast it lightly.
2. Melt butter, mix in garlic, and spread over the bread.
3. Toast for another 5 minutes and garnish with parsley.

Cost: $2.35 for 10-12 slices.

Mini Pizzas on English Muffins

Ingredients:

- 4 English muffins ($1.20)
- 1/2 cup tomato sauce ($0.40)
- 1/2 cup shredded cheese ($0.60)
- Optional toppings (pepperoni, veggies, etc.) ($0.50)

Instructions:

1. Cut the muffins in half, spread tomato sauce, add cheese and toppings.
2. Bake in the oven at 375ºF for 10 minutes.

Cost: $2.70 for 8 mini pizzas.

Veggie Sticks with Homemade Dip

Ingredients:

- 2 carrots ($0.50)
- 1 cucumber ($0.80)
- 1 celery stalk ($0.40)
- 1/4 cup sour cream ($0.30)
- 1 tablespoon mayonnaise ($0.10)
- 1 teaspoon garlic powder ($0.05)

Instructions:

1. Cut the veggies into sticks.
2. Mix sour cream, mayonnaise, and garlic powder to create a dip.

Cost: $2.15 for 4-5 servings.

Tomato and Basil Bruschetta

Ingredients:

- 1 small baguette ($1.00)
- 2 tomatoes ($0.80)
- 1 tablespoon olive oil ($0.20)
- Fresh basil (a few leaves) ($0.25)
- Salt and pepper to taste ($0.05)
- 4 bocconcini cheese balls cut in quarters ($0.70)

Instructions:

1. Dice tomatoes and toss them with olive oil, salt, and pepper.
2. Slice the baguette and toast the slices lightly.
3. Top each slice with the tomato mixture and garnish with fresh basil.

Cost: $3 for 10-12 servings.

Cheesy Garlic Breadsticks

Ingredients:

- 1 can refrigerated pizza dough ($1.50)
- 1/2 cup shredded mozzarella cheese ($0.80)
- 2 cloves garlic, minced ($0.10)
- 2 tablespoons butter ($0.20)

Instructions:

1. Roll out the pizza dough and brush with melted butter.
2. Sprinkle garlic and mozzarella over the dough.
3. Bake at 375°F for 12-15 minutes, then cut into sticks.

Cost: $2.60 for 8-10 breadsticks.

Hummus with Veggie Dippers

Ingredients:

- 1 can chickpeas ($0.80)
- 1 tablespoon tahini (optional) ($0.50)
- 1 tablespoon olive oil ($0.20)
- 1 clove garlic ($0.05)
- 2 carrots ($0.50)
- 1 cucumber ($0.80)

Instructions:

1. Blend chickpeas, tahini, olive oil, garlic, and a little water to make hummus.
2. Slice carrots and cucumber into sticks for dipping.

Cost: $2.85 for a small bowl of hummus and veggie sticks.

Baked Zucchini Fries

Ingredients:

- 2 zucchinis ($1.00)
- 1/2 cup breadcrumbs ($0.40)
- 1 egg ($0.20)
- Salt and pepper to taste ($0.05)

Instructions:

1. Slice zucchinis into fry-like shapes.
2. Dip each slice in beaten egg, then in breadcrumbs mixed with salt and pepper.
3. Bake at 400°F for 15-20 minutes until golden and crispy.

Cost: $1.65 for 2-3 servings.

Stuffed Mushrooms

Ingredients:

- 8-10 button mushrooms ($1.50)
- 2 tablespoons cream cheese ($0.30)
- 1 tablespoon breadcrumbs ($0.10)
- 1 tablespoon grated Parmesan cheese ($0.50)
- Salt and pepper to taste ($0.05)

Instructions:

1. Remove the mushroom stems and mix the cream cheese, breadcrumbs, Parmesan, salt, and pepper.
2. Stuff each mushroom cap with the mixture.
3. Bake at 350°F for 15-20 minutes.

Cost: $2.45 for 8-10 stuffed mushrooms.

Cheese and Cracker Bites

Ingredients:

- 1 box of crackers ($1.50)
- 4 slices of cheddar cheese ($1.00)
- 1 apple (optional for topping) ($0.50)
- Tuna fish (canned) ($3.50)

Instructions:

1. Slice the cheese into small squares.
2. Place cheese slices on top of crackers and add a thin slice of apple for extra flavor.

Cost: $3.00 for 12-15 bites.

Cucumber Sandwiches

Ingredients:

- 1 cucumber ($0.80)
- 4 slices of white bread ($0.60)
- 2 tablespoons cream cheese ($0.30)
- Salt and pepper to taste ($0.05)

Instructions:

1. Spread cream cheese onto slices of bread.
2. Peel and slice the cucumber thinly, place on bread, and sprinkle with salt and pepper.
3. Cut into bite-sized squares.

Cost: $1.75 for 4-6 sandwiches.

Garlic Parmesan Popcorn

Ingredients:

- 1/4 cup popcorn kernels ($0.50)
- 2 tablespoons butter ($0.20)
- 1 tablespoon grated Parmesan cheese ($0.50)
- 1 teaspoon garlic powder ($0.10)
- Salt to taste ($0.05)

Instructions:

1. **Pop the kernels:** If using a stovetop, heat a large pot over medium heat and add a tablespoon of oil. Once hot, add the popcorn kernels and cover the pot. Shake the pot occasionally to ensure even popping. If using a popcorn maker, follow the manufacturer's instructions.
2. **Melt the butter:** In a small saucepan over low heat, melt the butter until completely liquid. Alternatively, you can melt it in the microwave in a microwave-safe bowl in 15-second intervals.
3. **Combine:** Once the popcorn is popped, remove it from the heat. Drizzle the melted butter evenly over the popcorn. Sprinkle with grated Parmesan cheese, garlic powder, and salt.
4. **Toss:** Use a large spoon or your hands to toss the popcorn gently, ensuring the toppings are evenly distributed.

Cost: $1.35 for 4-5 servings.

Mini Quesadillas

Ingredients:

- 4 small flour tortillas ($0.80)
- 1/2 cup shredded cheese ($0.80)
- Salsa for dipping (optional) ($0.50)
- 2 T sour cream ($0.60)

Instructions:

1. **Prepare the tortillas:** Lay out the small flour tortillas on a flat surface. On one half of each tortilla, sprinkle an even layer of shredded cheese.
2. **Fold and cook:** Fold each tortilla in half to cover the cheese. Heat a non-stick skillet over medium heat and place the folded tortillas in the pan. Cook for about 2-3 minutes on each side until the tortillas are golden brown and the cheese is melted.
3. **Slice and serve:** Remove from the pan and allow to cool slightly. Slice each quesadilla into triangles and serve with salsa and sour cream on the side for dipping.

Cost: $2.70 for 4-6 mini quesadillas.

Grilled Eggplant and Red Pepper Skewers

Ingredients:

- 1 small eggplant ($1.25)
- 1 red bell pepper ($0.80)
- 1 tablespoon olive oil ($0.10)
- Salt and pepper to taste ($0.05)
- Wooden skewers for ($0.70)

Instructions:

1. **Prepare the vegetables:** Wash and dry the eggplant and red bell pepper. Cut the eggplant into 1-inch cubes and the red bell pepper into similar-sized chunks.
2. **Skewer the vegetables:** Thread the eggplant and bell pepper pieces onto skewers, alternating between the two.
3. **Season and grill:** Brush the skewers with olive oil and sprinkle with salt and pepper. Preheat a grill or grill pan over medium heat. Place the skewers on the grill and cook for about 6-8 minutes, turning occasionally, until the vegetables are tender and slightly charred.

Cost: $2.90 for 10 small skewers.

Roasted Eggplant and Bell Pepper Dip

Ingredients:

- 1 medium eggplant ($1.25)
- 1 green bell pepper ($0.75)
- 2 cloves garlic ($0.15)
- 1 tablespoon olive oil ($0.10)
- Salt and pepper to taste ($0.05)

Instructions:

1. **Roast the vegetables:** Preheat the oven to 400°F (200°C). Cut the eggplant and green bell pepper in half and place them cut-side down on a baking sheet. Roast for 20-25 minutes or until the skins are blistered and the flesh is soft.
2. **Prepare the dip:** Once roasted, allow the vegetables to cool slightly. Peel the skin off the eggplant and bell pepper. In a food processor, combine the roasted vegetables with minced garlic, olive oil, salt, and pepper. Blend until smooth and creamy.
3. **Serve:** Transfer the dip to a serving bowl and enjoy with crackers or fresh vegetables for dipping.

Cost: $2.30 for 4 servings.

Stuffed Mini Bell Peppers with Eggplant

Ingredients:

- 6 mini bell peppers ($0.90)
- 1/2 small eggplant, diced ($0.60)
- 1 tablespoon olive oil ($0.10)
- Salt and pepper to taste ($0.05)
- Mozzarella cheese 3 ounces ($1.00)

Instructions:

1. **Sauté the eggplant:** Heat olive oil in a skillet over medium heat. Add the diced eggplant and sauté for about 5 minutes or until it becomes tender. Season with salt and pepper to taste.
2. **Prepare the bell peppers:** While the eggplant is cooking, wash the mini bell peppers. Cut off the tops and remove the seeds.
3. **Stuff the peppers:** Once the eggplant is cooked, fill each mini bell pepper with the sautéed eggplant mixture.
4. **Roast:** Preheat the oven to 350ºF (175ºC) and place the stuffed peppers on a baking sheet. Roast for about 10 minutes until the peppers are slightly tender.

Cost: $2.65 for 6 stuffed peppers.

Eggplant and Bell Pepper Bruschetta

Ingredients:

- 1 small eggplant ($1.25)
- 1/2 red bell pepper, diced ($0.40)
- 1 tablespoon olive oil ($0.10)
- 1 small baguette ($0.75)
- Cream cheese ($2.50)

Instructions:

1. **Sauté the vegetables:** In a skillet over medium heat, heat the olive oil. Add the diced eggplant and red bell pepper and sauté until softened and slightly caramelized, about 5-7 minutes. Season with salt and pepper to taste.
2. **Prepare the baguette:** While the vegetables are cooking, slice the baguette into 1/2-inch thick pieces. Toast the slices on a baking sheet in the oven at 400ºF (200ºC) for about 5-7 minutes until lightly golden.
3. **Assemble and serve:** Top each toasted slice with the sautéed vegetable mixture. Drizzle with a bit more olive oil if desired, and serve warm.

Cost: $3.00 for 6-8 pieces.

Meatball Skewers

Ingredients:

- 1/2 lb ground beef ($1.75)
- 1 tablespoon breadcrumbs ($0.10)
- 1 egg ($0.20)
- Salt, pepper, and seasoning ($0.10)
- Sweet sauce bottles 1/4 cup ($0.50)

Instructions:

1. **Prepare the meat mixture:** In a large bowl, combine the ground beef, breadcrumbs, beaten egg, and your choice of seasonings (such as garlic powder, onion powder, or Italian seasoning). Mix until well combined.
2. **Form the meatballs:** Shape the mixture into small meatballs, about 1 inch in diameter.
3. **Cook the meatballs:** Heat a skillet over medium heat and add a little oil. Cook the meatballs until they are browned and cooked through, about 8-10 minutes, turning occasionally. Alternatively, you can bake them in a preheated oven at 375°F (190°C) for about 20 minutes.
4. **Serve on skewers:** Once cooked, let them cool slightly. Skewer the meatballs with toothpicks for easy serving.

Cost: $2.65 for 10-12 small meatballs.

Chicken Lettuce Wraps

Ingredients:

- 1/2 lb ground chicken ($1.50)
- 2 large lettuce leaves ($0.50)
- Soy sauce and seasoning ($0.25)
- 1 tablespoon diced onion ($0.15)
- Red onion minced, 1 Teaspoon ($0.20)
- 1 Sprig scallion diced ($.40)

Instructions:

1. **Cook the chicken:** In a skillet over medium heat, add the ground chicken and diced onion. Cook, breaking the meat apart with a spatula, until the chicken is fully cooked and no longer pink, about 5-7 minutes.
2. **Add seasoning:** Once the chicken is cooked, add soy sauce and any additional seasonings you like (such as ginger or garlic powder). Stir to combine and cook for another minute.
3. **Assemble the wraps:** Remove from heat. Spoon a generous amount of the chicken mixture into the center of each lettuce leaf. Roll the lettuce around the filling like a wrap.

Cost: $3.00 for 2-3 wraps.

Beef and Pepper Quesadillas

Ingredients:

- 1/4 lb ground beef ($0.90)
- 1/2 green bell pepper, diced ($0.35)
- 2 small tortillas ($0.60)
- 1 tablespoon shredded cheese ($0.25)

Instructions:

1. **Cook the filling:** In a skillet over medium heat, brown the ground beef. Add the diced green bell pepper and cook until the pepper is tender, about 3-4 minutes.
2. **Assemble the quesadillas:** Lay one tortilla flat in the skillet. Spread half of the beef and pepper mixture on one half of the tortilla, sprinkle with cheese, and fold the tortilla over to create a half-moon shape.
3. **Cook until crispy:** Cook for about 2-3 minutes on each side, or until the tortilla is crispy and the cheese has melted. Repeat with the second tortilla.

Cost: $2.10 for 2 quesadillas.

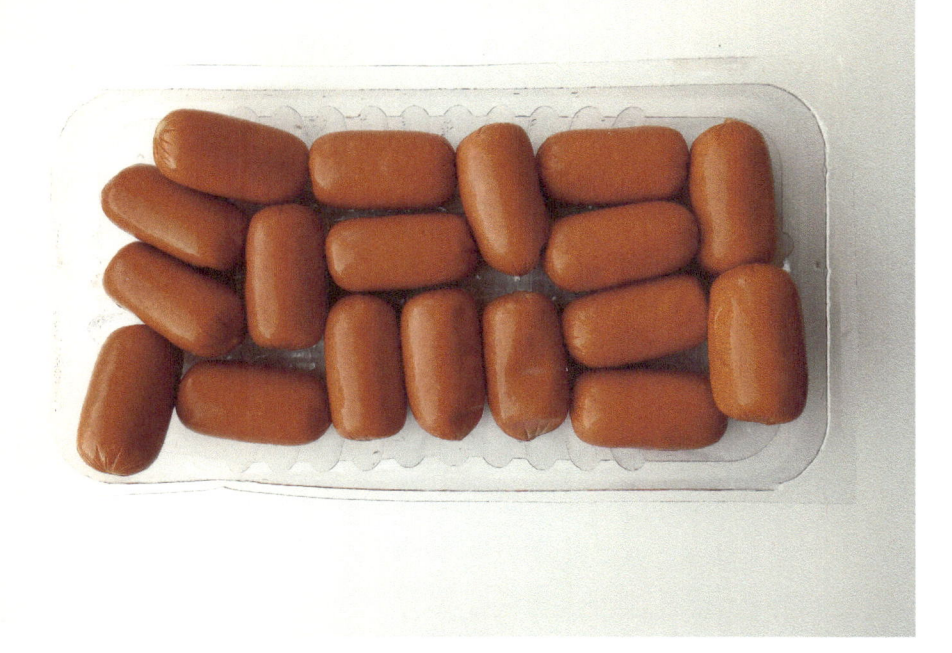

Mini Sausage Bites

Ingredients:
- 4 small breakfast sausages ($1.20)
- 1 tablespoon mustard ($0.10)
- 1 tablespoon honey ($0.20)

Instructions:
1. **Cook the sausages:** Start by heating a skillet over medium heat. Place the sausages in the skillet and cook them for about 6-8 minutes, turning them occasionally to ensure even browning. You want the sausages to be cooked through and golden brown on the outside.
2. **Slice the sausages:** Once browned, remove the sausages from the skillet and let them cool for a minute. Using a sharp knife, slice each sausage into bite-sized pieces, approximately 1-inch thick.
3. **Prepare the dipping sauce:** In a small bowl, combine the mustard and honey. Mix well until you have a smooth and creamy dipping sauce. Adjust the ratio of mustard and honey to your taste preference—add more honey for sweetness or more mustard for a tangy kick.
4. **Serve:** Arrange the sliced sausage bites on a serving platter. Serve the dipping sauce in a small bowl on the side for guests to dip their sausage bites. Enjoy your tasty mini sausage bites!

Cost: $1.50 for 4 servings.

Spicy Egg Salad with Avocado

Ingredients:

- 4 hard-boiled eggs ($0.80)
- 2 tablespoons mayonnaise ($0.20)
- 1 teaspoon Sriracha sauce ($0.10)
- 1/2 avocado, mashed ($0.50)
- 4 slices of whole grain bread ($0.60)

Instructions:

1. **Prepare the hard-boiled eggs:** If you haven't already, hard-boil the eggs by placing them in a pot, covering them with water, and bringing to a boil. Once boiling, remove from heat and cover for about 10-12 minutes. Afterward, transfer the eggs to an ice bath to cool, then peel and set aside.
2. **Make the egg salad mixture:** In a medium bowl, use a fork to mash the hard-boiled eggs until they are in small, even pieces. Add the mayonnaise, Sriracha sauce, and the mashed avocado. Mix well until all ingredients are fully incorporated. Adjust the Sriracha to your heat preference.
3. **Assemble the sandwiches:** Take two slices of whole grain bread and generously spread the egg salad mixture onto them. Top with the remaining two slices of bread to complete the sandwiches.
4. **Optional step:** For an added kick, consider adding sliced jalapeños on top of the egg salad before closing the sandwiches. This will enhance the spiciness and flavor.
5. **Serve and enjoy:** Cut the sandwiches in half if desired, and serve immediately. These sandwiches are perfect for a quick lunch or picnic!

Cost per sandwich: ~$1.75 (makes 2 sandwiches).

Peanut Butter & Nutty Banana Delight

Ingredients:
- 2 slices of whole wheat bread ($0.30)
- 2 tablespoons peanut butter ($0.15)
- 1 banana, sliced ($0.25)
- 1 tablespoon honey ($0.20)
- A sprinkle of cinnamon ($0.05)

Instructions:
1. **Spread the peanut butter:** Begin by taking two slices of whole wheat bread and laying them flat on a clean surface or plate. Use a butter knife to spread a generous layer of peanut butter evenly on one side of each slice.
2. **Prepare the banana:** Peel the banana and slice it into thin rounds. Ensure the slices are even to create a balanced texture in the sandwich.
3. **Layer the ingredients:** On top of the peanut butter of one slice, layer the banana slices evenly. Make sure to cover the peanut butter well for maximum flavor.
4. **Drizzle with honey:** Take the tablespoon of honey and drizzle it over the banana slices. This adds sweetness and a nice contrast to the nuttiness of the peanut butter.
5. **Add cinnamon:** Sprinkle a dash of cinnamon over the honey-drizzled bananas. This gives a lovely warmth and depth of flavor to the sandwich.
6. **Complete the sandwich:** Place the second slice of peanut butter-covered bread on top of the layered slice, peanut butter side down. Press gently to help the ingredients stick together.
7. **Slice and serve:** Cut the sandwich in half or quarters for easy eating. This delightful sandwich is great for lunch or a snack!

Cost per sandwich: ~$0.95.

Caprese Grilled Cheese

Ingredients:
- 2 slices of sourdough bread ($0.50)
- 1 slice of mozzarella cheese ($0.50)
- 2 slices of tomato ($0.25)
- Fresh basil leaves ($0.40)
- 1 tablespoon balsamic glaze ($0.30)
- 1 tablespoon butter ($0.10)

Instructions:
1. **Prepare the bread:** Start by laying out two slices of sourdough bread on a clean surface. Butter one side of each slice generously. This will create a golden, crispy crust when grilled.
2. **Layer the sandwich:** On the unbuttered side of one slice, layer the mozzarella cheese, followed by the tomato slices. Sprinkle a little salt and pepper on the tomatoes to enhance their flavor. Then, add fresh basil leaves on top.
3. **Add the balsamic glaze:** Drizzle balsamic glaze over the basil leaves and tomatoes for a sweet and tangy flavor that complements the cheese.
4. **Complete the sandwich:** Place the second slice of bread on top, buttered side facing out.
5. **Grill the sandwich:** Heat a non-stick skillet over medium heat. Once hot, carefully place the sandwich in the skillet. Grill for about 3-4 minutes on one side until golden brown. Use a spatula to press down gently on the sandwich for even grilling.
6. **Flip and continue grilling:** Carefully flip the sandwich and grill the other side for an additional 3-4 minutes, or until the cheese is melted and the bread is crispy.
7. **Serve:** Remove the sandwich from the skillet, let it cool slightly, and slice it in half. Serve warm, and enjoy the gooey, cheesy goodness!

Cost per sandwich: ~$2.05.

Mediterranean Hummus Wrap

Ingredients:
- 1 large whole wheat tortilla ($0.40)
- 3 tablespoons hummus ($0.30)
- 1/4 cucumber, sliced ($0.20)
- 1/4 bell pepper, sliced ($0.40)
- 5 olives, sliced ($0.30)
- Feta cheese, crumbled ($0.50)
- Leaf lettuce 2 leafs ($0.20)
- Avocado , ripe 1 half ($0.75)

Instructions:
1. **Prepare the tortilla:** Start by laying a large whole wheat tortilla flat on a clean surface. This will be the base for your wrap.
2. **Spread the hummus:** Use a spatula or the back of a spoon to spread 3 tablespoons of hummus evenly over the entire surface of the tortilla, leaving a little space around the edges.
3. **Add the fresh vegetables:** Begin layering the sliced cucumber and bell pepper on top of the hummus. Distribute them evenly across the tortilla for balanced flavor and crunch.
4. **Incorporate olives and feta:** Next, add the sliced olives and sprinkle crumbled feta cheese over the vegetables. The olives add a briny flavor, while the feta brings creaminess and tang.
5. **Roll the wrap:** Starting from one end, carefully roll the tortilla tightly over the filling, tucking in the sides as you go to prevent the filling from spilling out.
6. **Slice and serve:** Once rolled, use a sharp knife to slice the wrap in half. Serve immediately for a fresh and flavorful lunch option.

Cost per sandwich: ~$2.85

Sweet and Savory Tuna Melt

Ingredients:

- 1 can of tuna ($1.00)
- 1 tablespoon mayonnaise ($0.10)
- 1 tablespoon sweet pickle relish ($0.15)
- 1 slice of cheddar cheese ($0.50)
- 2 slices of bread ($0.30)

Instructions:

1. **Prepare the tuna:** Open the can of tuna and drain it thoroughly. Place the drained tuna in a medium mixing bowl.
2. **Mix the ingredients:** Add the mayonnaise and sweet pickle relish to the bowl with the tuna. Use a fork to mix everything together until well combined. You want a creamy consistency that's spreadable.
3. **Assemble the sandwich:** Take one slice of bread and spread a generous amount of the tuna mixture over it. Place a slice of cheddar cheese on top of the tuna.
4. **Complete the sandwich:** Top with the second slice of bread to complete the sandwich.
5. **Grill or toast the sandwich:** Preheat a non-stick skillet or pan over medium heat. Add a little butter or oil to the pan if desired. Place the sandwich in the pan and grill for about 3-4 minutes on one side until golden brown.
6. **Flip and continue cooking:** Carefully flip the sandwich and grill the other side for another 3-4 minutes until the cheese melts and the bread is golden.
7. **Serve:** Remove the sandwich from the heat, let it cool for a minute, then slice it in half. Serve warm and enjoy the sweet and savory flavors!

Cost per sandwich: ~$2.05 (makes 2 sandwiches).

Savory Breakfast Sandwich

Ingredients:

- 1 egg ($0.20)
- 1 slice of cheese ($0.50)
- 1 slice of ham or turkey ($0.60)
- 1 English muffin or bagel ($0.50)
- A dab of mustard or hot sauce ($0.10)

Instructions:

1. **Cook the egg:** Heat a non-stick skillet over medium heat. Crack the egg into the skillet and cook it to your desired doneness—sunny side up, scrambled, or over easy. Season with salt and pepper to taste.
2. **Toast the English muffin or bagel:** While the egg is cooking, split the English muffin or bagel in half and toast it in a toaster or on a pan until golden brown.
3. **Assemble the sandwich:** Once the egg is cooked, place the slice of cheese on top of the egg in the skillet to let it melt slightly. On the bottom half of the toasted English muffin or bagel, layer the egg with melted cheese and add the slice of ham or turkey on top.
4. **Add the condiment:** Finish by adding a dab of mustard or hot sauce to the top half of the English muffin or bagel before closing the sandwich.
5. **Serve:** Place the top half of the muffin or bagel on the sandwich, press down gently, and serve immediately. This hearty breakfast sandwich is perfect for a quick meal!

Cost per sandwich: ~$1.90.

Mediterranean Pita Pocket

Ingredients:

- 1 whole wheat pita ($0.50)
- 1/4 cup chickpeas, mashed ($0.30)
- 1/4 cucumber, diced ($0.20)
- 1 tablespoon tahini ($0.30)
- Handful of spinach or lettuce ($0.40)
- Cherry tomatoes halved 4, ($0.60)

Instructions:

1. **Prepare the Chickpea Spread**: In a mixing bowl, add the mashed chickpeas. You can use a fork or a potato masher to mash them until they are creamy but still have some texture. Stir in the tahini until well combined. This will create a flavorful and creamy spread that serves as the base for your pita pocket.
2. **Prepare the Vegetables:** Dice the cucumber into small pieces. If you're using spinach or lettuce, rinse them under cold water and pat them dry with a paper towel. This ensures your vegetables are fresh and crunchy.
3. **Assemble the Pita:** Carefully cut the whole wheat pita in half to create two pockets. Take one half and gently open it up. Spread a generous amount of the chickpea mixture inside the pita pocket, making sure to cover the bottom evenly.
4. **Add Fresh Ingredients:** Stuff the pita with the diced cucumber and a handful of spinach or lettuce. You can adjust the amount of filling based on your preference.
5. **Add Optional Toppings:** If desired, sprinkle a pinch of paprika or drizzle a little lemon juice over the filling for added flavor and freshness.
6. **Serve:** Once filled, close the pita pocket gently and enjoy your Mediterranean meal. This dish can be served as a light lunch or a snack.

Cost: ~$2.30

Apple and Cheddar Grilled Sandwich

Ingredients:

- 2 slices of whole-grain bread ($0.40)
- 1/2 apple, thinly sliced ($0.25)
- 1 slice of cheddar cheese ($0.50)
- 1 tablespoon butter ($0.10)
- 2 slices of ham ($1.00)

Instructions:

1. **Prepare the Bread:** Start by taking two slices of whole-grain bread and laying them flat on a clean surface or cutting board.
2. **Butter the Bread:** Spread butter on one side of each slice. This will help achieve a golden, crispy texture when grilling.
3. **Layer the Ingredients:** On the unbuttered side of one slice, lay the thin apple slices evenly. Make sure to distribute them to cover the bread adequately. Next, place the slice of cheddar cheese on top of the apple slices. The cheese should be slightly overlapping the apples for better melting.
4. **Top and Grill:** Place the second slice of bread on top, buttered side up. Preheat a skillet or frying pan over medium heat. Carefully place the sandwich in the pan. Grill for about 3-4 minutes on each side, pressing down gently with a spatula, until the bread is golden brown and the cheese has melted.
5. **Serve:** Once cooked, remove the sandwich from the pan and let it cool for a minute. Cut it in half and serve warm. Enjoy the combination of sweet apples and savory cheddar cheese!

Cost: ~$2.25

Spicy Black Bean & Avocado Wrap

Ingredients:
- 1 large tortilla ($0.40)
- 1/2 can of black beans, rinsed and mashed ($0.60)
- 1/2 avocado, sliced ($0.50)
- Salsa (2 tablespoons) ($0.20)
- 1 cup scrambled eggs ($0.80)
- 1 pinch cayenne pepper ($0.10)

Instructions:
1. **Prepare the Tortilla:** Lay the large tortilla flat on a clean surface. If desired, warm it slightly in a pan or microwave to make it more pliable.
2. **Mash the Black Beans:** In a small bowl, take the rinsed black beans and use a fork to mash them until they reach a creamy consistency, leaving some chunks for texture.
3. **Spread the Beans:** Spread the mashed black beans evenly over the tortilla, leaving a little space at the edges to prevent overflow when rolling.
4. **Add Avocado and Salsa:** Lay the slices of avocado on top of the black beans, and then add 2 tablespoons of salsa evenly over the avocado.
5. **Roll the Wrap:** Starting from one edge, carefully roll the tortilla tightly around the filling, tucking in the sides as you go to secure the contents. Once rolled, you can slice the wrap in half for easier handling.
6. **Serve:** Enjoy your spicy black bean and avocado wrap as a quick lunch or snack. It's packed with flavor and nutrition!

Cost: ~$2.60

Caprese Skewers Sandwich

Ingredients:

- 2 slices of baguette or French bread ($0.50)
- 4 cherry tomatoes ($0.30)
- 1/4 cup mozzarella balls ($0.80)
- Fresh basil leaves ($0.40)
- Balsamic vinegar drizzle ($0.10)

Instructions:

1. **Prepare the Baguette:** Slice the baguette or French bread into two pieces, approximately 4-6 inches long, depending on your preference. You can toast the slices lightly if desired.
2. **Assemble the Skewers:** On small skewers or toothpicks, thread the cherry tomatoes, mozzarella balls, and fresh basil leaves. Alternate the ingredients for a colorful presentation.
3. **Toast the Bread:** If not already toasted, place the slices of baguette in a toaster or under a broiler for a few minutes until lightly golden and crisp.
4. **Serve the Skewers:** Place the assembled skewers on top of the toasted baguette slices. Drizzle balsamic vinegar over the skewers for an added tangy flavor.
5. **Enjoy:** Serve the Caprese skewers immediately while the bread is warm. This dish makes a fantastic appetizer or light lunch.

Cost: ~$2.20

Vegetable Fried Rice

Ingredients:

- 2 cups cooked rice ($0.40)
- 1 cup mixed frozen vegetables ($0.50)
- 1 egg, beaten ($0.20)
- 2 tablespoons soy sauce ($0.20)
- 1 tablespoon oil for frying ($0.10)
- Green onions (optional) ($0.20)
- 1 teaspoon honey ($0.25)

Instructions:

1. **Heat the Oil:** In a large frying pan or wok, heat the oil over medium heat. Ensure the oil is hot before adding any ingredients.
2. **Cook the Vegetables:** Add the mixed frozen vegetables to the pan. Stir-fry them for about 3-5 minutes or until they are heated through and tender. You can add a little salt and pepper for additional flavor during this step.
3. **Scramble the Egg:** Push the vegetables to one side of the pan. Pour the beaten egg into the empty side and scramble it until fully cooked. Combine the egg with the vegetables once cooked.
4. **Add Rice and Sauce:** Add the cooked rice to the pan. Pour in the soy sauce and mix everything together thoroughly. Stir-fry for an additional 2-3 minutes, allowing the rice to heat up and absorb the flavors.
5. **Garnish and Serve:** If using, chop the green onions and sprinkle them over the fried rice just before serving. Mix gently and serve hot. Enjoy this versatile dish as a main course or side!

Cost: ~$1.95

Chickpea Salad

Ingredients:

- 1 can chickpeas, rinsed and drained ($0.80)
- 1/2 cucumber, diced ($0.20)
- 1/4 red onion, diced ($0.20)
- 1 tablespoon olive oil ($0.20)
- 1 tablespoon lemon juice ($0.10)
- Salt and pepper to taste ($0.10)

Instructions:

1. **Prepare the Ingredients:** Open the can of chickpeas and rinse them under cold water to remove any excess sodium. Drain well. Dice the cucumber and red onion into small pieces for easy mixing.
2. **Combine Ingredients:** In a large bowl, add the rinsed chickpeas, diced cucumber, and red onion. Use a spatula or spoon to gently combine the ingredients, being careful not to mash the chickpeas too much.
3. **Dress the Salad:** Drizzle the olive oil and lemon juice over the salad. Sprinkle salt and pepper to taste.
4. **Toss and Serve:** Gently toss the salad to ensure all ingredients are well-coated in the dressing. Serve immediately for the freshest taste, or refrigerate for 30 minutes for the flavors to meld together.
5. **Enjoy:** This chickpea salad can be served on its own, as a filling in pita bread, or as a side dish.

Cost: ~$1.70

Pasta Primavera

Ingredients:

- 2 cups pasta of your choice ($0.50)
- 1 cup mixed seasonal vegetables (like bell peppers, zucchini) ($0.80)
- 2 tablespoons olive oil ($0.20)
- 1 clove garlic, minced ($0.10)
- Salt and pepper to taste ($0.10)
- 1/2 teaspoon dijon mustard. ($0.20)

Instructions:

1. **Cook the Pasta:** In a large pot, bring salted water to a boil. Add the pasta and cook according to package instructions until al dente. Drain the pasta and set aside, reserving a little pasta water for later if needed.
2. **Sauté the Vegetables:** In a large skillet, heat the olive oil over medium heat. Add the minced garlic and sauté for about 30 seconds until fragrant. Then add the mixed seasonal vegetables and sauté for 5-7 minutes or until they are tender but still crisp.
3. **Combine Pasta and Vegetables:** Add the cooked pasta to the skillet with the sautéed vegetables. Toss everything together, adding a splash of the reserved pasta water if needed to help combine.
4. **Season:** Season with salt and pepper to taste. Toss again to ensure even seasoning throughout the dish.
5. **Serve:** Serve the pasta primavera hot, garnished with freshly grated Parmesan cheese if desired. This dish is colorful and packed with nutrients!

Cost: ~$1.90

Sweet Potato and Black Bean Tacos

Ingredients:
- 1 medium sweet potato, diced ($0.50)
- 1/2 can black beans, rinsed and drained ($0.60)
- 2 corn tortillas ($0.40)
- 1 tablespoon olive oil ($0.20)
- Salsa for topping ($0.20)
- Salt and pepper to taste ($0.10)
- 2 Tablespoons grate parmesan cheese ($0.60)

Instructions:
1. **Preheat Oven:** Preheat your oven to 425°F (220°C). This will ensure the sweet potato is nicely roasted.
2. **Roast Sweet Potato:** Toss the diced sweet potato in olive oil and season with salt and pepper. Spread the sweet potato evenly on a baking sheet and roast in the preheated oven for about 20-25 minutes, or until fork-tender and slightly caramelized.
3. **Prepare the Beans:** While the sweet potato is roasting, rinse and drain the black beans. You can warm them in a small saucepan over medium heat for about 5 minutes, stirring occasionally.
4. **Assemble the Tacos:** Once the sweet potato is cooked, take the corn tortillas and warm them in a separate pan for about 30 seconds on each side, or until soft. Fill each tortilla with a generous scoop of roasted sweet potato and black beans.
5. **Add Toppings:** Top the tacos with salsa and any other desired toppings, like avocado or cilantro.
6. **Serve:** Enjoy your sweet potato and black bean tacos while they're warm. These tacos are not only delicious but also packed with nutrients!

Cost: ~$2.60

Vegetable Egg Foo Young

Ingredients:

- 2 cups mixed vegetables (frozen or fresh) - ($0.80)
- 4 eggs - ($0.80)
- 2 tablespoons soy sauce - ($0.10)
- 1 tablespoon vegetable oil - ($0.10)
- 2 scallions, chopped - ($0.20)
- 1/4 cup brown gravy (store-bought or homemade) - optional ($0.50)
- Salt and pepper to taste (optional)
- 4 shrimp small - ($0.50)

Instructions:

1. **Prepare vegetables:** Heat the vegetable oil in a large pan over medium heat. Add the mixed vegetables and cook for 3-4 minutes, until softened. Set aside to cool slightly.
2. **Whisk eggs:** In a bowl, beat the eggs, soy sauce, and half of the chopped scallions. Mix in the cooked vegetables.
3. **Cook egg mixture:** In the same pan, pour the egg mixture and cook it like an omelet for 2-3 minutes on each side, until both sides are golden brown and cooked through.
4. **Heat gravy (optional):** While the egg foo young cooks, warm up the brown gravy if you're using it.
5. **Serve:** Plate the egg foo young, drizzle with optional brown gravy, and garnish with the remaining scallions.

Total Cost: ~$2.50 - $3.00 depending on gravy usage.

Stir-Fried Cabbage and Carrots

Ingredients:

- 1/2 head cabbage, sliced ($0.50)
- 2 carrots, julienned ($0.30)
- 2 tablespoons soy sauce ($0.10)
- 1 tablespoon sesame oil ($0.15)
- 1 teaspoon ginger, minced ($0.05)
- Salt and pepper to taste .10
- Chinese 5 sice .23

Instructions:

1. **Prepare Vegetables:** Slice the cabbage and julienne the carrots, ensuring they are cut into even sizes for uniform cooking.
2. **Heat Oil:** In a large skillet or wok, heat the sesame oil over medium-high heat.
3. **Add Vegetables:** Add the sliced cabbage and julienned carrots to the skillet. Stir-fry for about 5-7 minutes, stirring frequently until the vegetables are tender but still crisp.
4. **Season:** Add the soy sauce and minced ginger, tossing everything together to coat the vegetables. Cook for an additional 1-2 minutes.
5. **Serve:** Transfer the stir-fried cabbage and carrots to a serving dish and enjoy as a healthy side!

Total Cost: ~$1.43

Greek Pasta Salad

Ingredients:
- 8 oz pasta ($0.75)
- 1/2 cup olives ($0.70)
- 1/2 cup feta cheese, crumbled ($0.50)
- 1/2 cup cherry tomatoes ($0.80)
- 2 tablespoons olive oil ($0.20)
- 1 pinch dried organo ($0.50)

Instructions:
1. **Cook the Pasta:** Begin by bringing a large pot of salted water to a boil. Add the pasta and cook according to the package instructions until al dente. This usually takes about 8-10 minutes. Once cooked, drain the pasta in a colander and rinse under cold water to stop the cooking process. This helps cool the pasta and prevents it from becoming mushy.
2. **Prepare the Ingredients:** While the pasta is cooling, prepare the other ingredients. If the olives are whole, slice them into halves or quarters for easier eating. For the cherry tomatoes, wash them thoroughly and cut them in half. If the feta cheese is in a block, crumble it into bite-sized pieces using your hands or a fork.
3. **Combine the Ingredients:** In a large mixing bowl, combine the cooled pasta, olives, crumbled feta cheese, and halved cherry tomatoes. Ensure that the ingredients are evenly distributed throughout the salad.
4. **Dress the Salad:** Drizzle the olive oil over the pasta mixture. Using a large spoon or spatula, gently toss everything together until well combined. Be careful not to break the feta cheese too much; you want to maintain some chunks for texture.
5. **Taste and Adjust:** Before serving, taste the salad. You can add a pinch of salt or a splash of additional olive oil if needed, depending on your taste preference. If you like a bit of acidity, consider adding a squeeze of fresh lemon juice.
6. **Serve:** This salad can be served immediately, but for best flavor, let it sit in the refrigerator for about 30 minutes to an hour. This allows the flavors to meld together beautifully. Serve chilled or at room temperature.

Total Cost: ~$1.43

Greek Lemon Rice Soup (Avgolemono)

Ingredients:

- 1/2 cup rice ($0.25)
- 4 cups vegetable broth ($1.00)
- 2 eggs ($0.30)
- 1 lemon, juiced ($0.50)
- Salt and pepper to taste ($0.05)

Instructions:

1. **Cook the Rice:** In a medium-sized pot, bring the vegetable broth to a gentle boil. Add the rice and reduce the heat to low. Cover the pot and let the rice simmer for about 15-20 minutes, or until tender. Stir occasionally to prevent the rice from sticking to the bottom of the pot.
2. **Prepare the Egg-Lemon Mixture:** While the rice is cooking, crack the eggs into a medium bowl. Using a whisk or fork, beat the eggs until they are well mixed. Gradually add the lemon juice to the eggs while whisking continuously to combine. This will create a smooth mixture.
3. **Temper the Egg Mixture:** Once the rice is cooked, take a ladle of hot broth from the pot and slowly pour it into the egg mixture while whisking vigorously. This step is crucial to prevent the eggs from curdling when added to the soup. Continue adding a few more ladles of hot broth, whisking all the while until the mixture is warm.
4. **Combine and Heat:** Pour the egg-lemon mixture back into the pot with the remaining broth and rice. Stir gently to combine everything. Place the pot back on low heat and warm the soup gently. Avoid boiling it at this stage to keep the eggs from scrambling.
5. **Season to Taste:** Once the soup is heated through, taste and season with salt and pepper to your liking. You can also add a little more lemon juice for extra tanginess if desired.
6. **Serve:** Ladle the soup into bowls and enjoy it warm. It pairs wonderfully with crusty bread or a side salad.

Total Cost: ~$2.10

Vegetable Quesadillas

Ingredients:

- 4 flour tortillas ($1.00)
- 1 cup mixed vegetables (bell peppers, onions, corn) ($0.70)
- 1 cup shredded cheese ($1.00)
- 1 Teaspoon oil ($0.25)
- Salt and paper to taste ($0.50)

Instructions:

1. **Prepare the Vegetables:** If using fresh vegetables, wash and chop them into small, uniform pieces. If using frozen vegetables, thaw them in a microwave or on the stovetop until heated through.
2. **Heat the Skillet:** Preheat a large skillet over medium heat. Add a little oil if desired, but the cheese will help with sticking if you're using a non-stick pan.
3. **Assemble the Quesadilla:** Place one tortilla in the skillet. Sprinkle about 1/4 of the shredded cheese evenly over the tortilla, followed by a generous layer of mixed vegetables. Top with another tortilla.
4. **Cook the Quesadilla:** Allow the quesadilla to cook for about 2-3 minutes or until the bottom is golden brown and the cheese begins to melt. Carefully flip the quesadilla using a spatula. Cook for an additional 2-3 minutes on the other side until golden and the cheese is fully melted.
5. **Cut and Serve:** Remove the quesadilla from the skillet and place it on a cutting board. Let it cool for a minute before cutting into wedges. Repeat the process with the remaining tortillas and filling. Serve with salsa, sour cream, or guacamole for dipping.

Total Cost: ~$2.95

Mexican Rice

Ingredients:

- 1 cup long-grain rice ($0.30)
- 1/2 cup tomato sauce ($0.50)
- 2 cups vegetable broth or water ($0.50)
- 1/2 onion, chopped ($0.20)
- Spices (cumin, salt) to taste ($0.10)

Instructions:

1. **Sauté the Onions:** In a medium saucepan, heat a splash of oil over medium heat. Add the chopped onion and sauté until translucent and fragrant, about 3-5 minutes. This will enhance the flavor of your rice.
2. **Add the Rice:** Add the long-grain rice to the pot and stir well to coat it in the oil and onions. Sauté the rice for about 2-3 minutes, stirring constantly. This step helps toasting the rice, adding a nutty flavor.
3. **Add Tomato Sauce and Broth:** Pour in the tomato sauce and stir to combine. Gradually add the vegetable broth or water, bringing the mixture to a boil.
4. **Simmer the Rice:** Once boiling, reduce the heat to low, cover the pot, and let it simmer for about 20 minutes or until the rice is tender and has absorbed the liquid. Avoid lifting the lid too often, as this can release steam and prolong cooking time.
5. **Season and Fluff:** After the cooking time, remove the pot from heat. Let it sit covered for an additional 5 minutes. Then, remove the lid, fluff the rice with a fork, and season with cumin, salt, and any other spices you like.
6. **Serve:** Serve the Mexican rice as a side dish or as a base for your favorite Mexican-inspired meals.

Total Cost: ~$1.60

Bean and Cheese Burritos

Ingredients:

- 4 flour tortillas ($1.00)
- 1 can refried beans ($0.80)
- 1 cup shredded cheese ($1.00)

Instructions:

1. **Prepare the Filling:** Open the can of refried beans and heat them in a small saucepan over low heat, stirring occasionally until warmed through. This will make them easier to spread.
2. **Warm the Tortillas:** If desired, you can warm the tortillas briefly in a skillet or microwave for about 10-15 seconds to make them more pliable. This helps prevent tearing when rolling.
3. **Assemble the Burritos:** Lay a tortilla flat on a clean surface. Spread about 1/4 of the refried beans evenly across the center of the tortilla, leaving a little space on the edges. Sprinkle a generous amount of shredded cheese over the beans.
4. **Roll the Burritos:** Fold in the sides of the tortilla over the filling, then roll from the bottom up, tucking in the sides as you go to create a tight roll. Repeat this process with the remaining tortillas.
5. **Bake the Burritos:** Place the rolled burritos seam-side down on a baking sheet. Preheat your oven to 350°F (175°C). Bake the burritos for about 10-15 minutes or until heated through and the cheese is melted.
6. **Serve:** Cut the burritos in half if desired and serve warm with salsa or guacamole.

Total Cost: ~$2.80

Mexican Street Corn Salad (Esquites)

Ingredients:

- 2 cups frozen corn ($0.80)
- 1/4 cup mayonnaise ($0.25)
- 1/4 cup cotija cheese ($0.80)
- 1 lime, juiced ($0.50)
- Chili powder and salt to taste ($0.15)

Instructions:

1. **Cook the Corn:** In a large skillet, heat over medium-high heat. Add the frozen corn and cook, stirring occasionally, until the corn is heated through and slightly charred, about 5-7 minutes. This step adds a smoky flavor to your salad.
2. **Prepare the Dressing:** In a separate mixing bowl, combine the mayonnaise, lime juice, and a pinch of salt. Whisk together until smooth.
3. **Combine Ingredients:** Once the corn is cooked, remove it from the heat and let it cool slightly. In a large bowl, combine the charred corn with the mayonnaise mixture. Stir to combine thoroughly.
4. **Add Cheese and Season:** Fold in the cotija cheese and sprinkle chili powder to taste. Adjust the seasoning according to your preference.
5. **Serve:** You can serve this dish warm, at room temperature, or chilled. It makes a great side dish for barbecues or taco nights!

Total Cost: ~$2.50

Chilaquiles

Ingredients:
- 2 cups tortilla chips ($1.00)
- 1 cup salsa ($0.75)
- 1/2 cup cheese ($0.75)
- Optional: 1 egg, fried ($0.25)

Instructions:
1. **Prepare the Salsa:** In a skillet over medium heat, pour in the salsa and allow it to heat through for about 2-3 minutes. Stir occasionally to prevent sticking and ensure even heating.
2. **Add Tortilla Chips:** Once the salsa is warm, gently add the tortilla chips into the skillet. Using a spatula, stir the chips to coat them evenly with the salsa. Cook for an additional 2-4 minutes, allowing the chips to absorb some of the salsa while becoming slightly softened but still retaining some crunch.
3. **Melt the Cheese:** Sprinkle the cheese over the top of the tortilla chips. Reduce the heat to low and cover the skillet with a lid for about 1-2 minutes. This will trap heat and steam, helping the cheese to melt evenly.
4. **Prepare the Egg (Optional):** If you choose to add a fried egg, heat a small frying pan over medium heat. Crack the egg into the pan and cook to your desired doneness, whether that's sunny-side-up or over-easy. This typically takes about 2-3 minutes.
5. **Serve:** Once the cheese is melted and the egg is cooked, plate the chilaquiles by spooning them onto a serving dish. Top with the fried egg if using, and feel free to garnish with additional salsa, avocado, or cilantro if desired. Serve immediately for the best flavor and texture.

Total Cost: ~$2.50

Basic Risotto

Ingredients:

- 1 cup Arborio rice ($1.00)
- 4 cups vegetable broth ($1.00)
- 1 small onion, diced ($0.30)
- 1/4 cup grated Parmesan cheese ($0.75)
- Salt and pepper to taste ($0.05)

Instructions:

1. **Sauté the Onion:** In a large saucepan or deep skillet, heat a tablespoon of olive oil over medium heat. Once hot, add the diced onion and sauté for about 4-5 minutes, or until it becomes translucent and fragrant, stirring occasionally to prevent burning.
2. **Add Arborio Rice:** Pour in the Arborio rice and stir it into the onions. Toast the rice for about 2-3 minutes, stirring constantly to coat the grains with oil and to lightly toast them, which enhances their nutty flavor.
3. **Gradually Add Broth:** Start adding the vegetable broth, one ladle at a time, while continuously stirring. Wait for the rice to absorb most of the liquid before adding the next ladle. This process takes about 18-20 minutes. The rice should be creamy and al dente when finished.
4. **Stir in Cheese and Season:** Once the risotto reaches the desired consistency, remove it from heat. Stir in the grated Parmesan cheese, mixing well until it is melted and incorporated. Season with salt and pepper to taste, adjusting according to your preference.
5. **Serve:** Spoon the risotto into bowls, and optionally garnish with more cheese or fresh herbs. Serve warm as a main dish or a side.

Total Cost: ~$3.10

Mushroom Risotto

Ingredients:

- 1 cup Arborio rice ($0.50)
- 4 cups vegetable broth ($0.50)
- 1 cup mushrooms, sliced ($0.43)
- 1 small onion, diced ($0.30)
- 1/4 cup grated Parmesan cheese ($0.75)
- Salt and pepper to taste ($0.05)

Instructions:

1. **Sauté Onions and Mushrooms:** In a large skillet, heat a tablespoon of olive oil over medium heat. Add the diced onion and cook for about 3-4 minutes until it becomes translucent. Add the sliced mushrooms and cook for another 5-7 minutes until they are soft and browned, stirring occasionally.
2. **Add Arborio Rice:** Once the mushrooms are cooked, stir in the Arborio rice. Cook for about 2-3 minutes, stirring frequently, allowing the rice to absorb the flavors of the mushrooms and onions.
3. **Gradually Add Broth:** Begin adding the vegetable broth one ladle at a time, stirring constantly. Allow the rice to absorb most of the liquid before adding more. Continue this process until the rice is creamy and tender, which should take about 18-20 minutes.
4. **Stir in Cheese and Season:** Once cooked, remove the skillet from the heat. Stir in the grated Parmesan cheese until melted and creamy. Season with salt and pepper to taste.
5. **Serve:** Spoon the mushroom risotto into bowls and garnish with additional Parmesan cheese or fresh herbs. Serve warm as a comforting meal.

Total Cost: ~$2.53

Spinach and Feta Risotto

Ingredients:

- 1/2 cup Arborio rice – $0.50
- 4 cups chicken broth (instead of vegetable) – $0.50
- 1/2 cup cooked, shredded chicken breast – $0.50
- 1/2 cup spinach, chopped – $0.25
- 2 tablespoons feta cheese, crumbled – $0.30
- 1/2 small onion, diced – $0.15
- Salt and pepper to taste – $0.05

Instructions:

1. **Cook the Onions:** In a large saucepan, heat a tablespoon of olive oil over medium heat. Add the diced onion and cook for about 4-5 minutes until translucent.
2. **Add Arborio Rice:** Stir in the Arborio rice and toast it for 2-3 minutes, stirring frequently to coat the rice with oil and heat it through.
3. **Gradually Add Broth:** Add the vegetable broth one ladle at a time, stirring continuously. Wait for the rice to absorb most of the liquid before adding more. This should take about 18-20 minutes until the rice is creamy and al dente.
4. **Incorporate Spinach and Feta:** When the risotto is nearly done, fold in the chopped spinach and let it wilt into the rice. Remove from heat and stir in the crumbled feta cheese, allowing it to melt slightly. Season with salt and pepper to taste.
5. **Serve:** Plate the risotto and garnish with additional feta or fresh herbs if desired. Serve warm for a deliciously creamy dish.

Total Cost: ~$2.25

Beef and Tomato Risotto

Ingredients:

- 1/2 cup Arborio rice – $0.50
- 4 cups vegetable broth – $0.50
- 1/4 cup cooked, shredded beef – $0.75
- 1/2 can diced tomatoes – $0.40
- 1/2 small onion, diced – $0.15
- Salt and pepper to taste – $0.05

Instructions:

1. **Sauté Onions:** In a large pot or deep skillet, heat a tablespoon of olive oil over medium heat. Add the diced onion and sauté for about 4-5 minutes until soft and translucent.
2. **Add Arborio Rice:** Stir in the Arborio rice, toasting it for about 2-3 minutes while stirring frequently. This step helps to bring out the rice's nutty flavor.
3. **Add Tomatoes and Gradually Broth:** Pour in the can of diced tomatoes (including the juice) and stir well. Begin adding the vegetable broth one ladle at a time, stirring continuously until the rice absorbs most of the liquid before adding more. This process should take around 18-20 minutes until the rice is creamy and cooked through.
4. **Season:** Once the risotto is cooked, remove it from heat and season with salt and pepper to taste.
5. **Serve:** Spoon the tomato risotto into bowls, and garnish with fresh herbs or additional Parmesan cheese if desired. Serve warm as a satisfying meal.

Total Cost: ~$2.35

Pea and Mint Risotto

Ingredients:

- 1/2 cup Arborio rice – $0.50
- 3 cups vegetable broth – $0.75
- 1/2 cup frozen peas – $0.40
- 1/2 small onion, diced – $0.15
- 1 tablespoon fresh mint, chopped – $0.15
- Salt and pepper to taste – $0.05

Instructions:

1. **Cook the Onions:** Heat a tablespoon of olive oil in a large pot over medium heat. Add the diced onion and sauté for about 4-5 minutes, or until soft and translucent.
2. **Add Arborio Rice:** Stir in the Arborio rice and toast it for 2-3 minutes, stirring frequently to ensure all grains are well-coated with oil.
3. **Gradually Stir in Broth:** Begin adding the vegetable broth one ladle at a time, stirring constantly until the rice absorbs most of the liquid before adding more. This should take about 18-20 minutes until the rice is creamy and tender.
4. **Add Peas and Mint:** When the risotto is nearly done cooking, stir in the frozen peas and fresh mint. Continue to cook for an additional 2-3 minutes until the peas are heated through.
5. **Serve:** Remove from heat and season with salt and pepper to taste. Serve the risotto warm, garnished with additional mint if desired.

Total Cost: ~$2.00

Lemon Basil Garlic Spaghetti

Ingredients:

- 8 oz spaghetti – $0.50
- 4 cloves garlic, minced – $0.30
- 1/4 cup olive oil – $0.75
- 1/2 cup fresh basil, chopped – $0.50
- Zest of 1 lemon – $0.25
- Salt and pepper to taste – $0.05
- Optional: crushed red pepper flakes – $0.05

Instructions:

1. **Cook Spaghetti:** Bring a large pot of salted water to a boil. Add the spaghetti and cook according to package instructions until al dente, usually about 8-10 minutes. Reserve 1/2 cup of pasta water, then drain the pasta.
2. **Sauté Garlic:** While the pasta is cooking, heat the olive oil in a large skillet over medium heat. Add the minced garlic and sauté for about 1-2 minutes until fragrant, but be careful not to burn it.
3. **Add Spinach:** Stir in the fresh spinach and cook for another 2-3 minutes until wilted. If desired, add crushed red pepper flakes for a bit of heat.
4. **Combine Pasta:** Add the drained spaghetti to the skillet along with the reserved pasta water. Toss everything together to combine well, cooking for an additional 1-2 minutes.
5. **Add Lemon Zest and Season:** Remove the skillet from heat and stir in the lemon zest. Season with salt and pepper to taste.
6. **Serve:** Plate the pasta warm, garnishing with additional lemon zest or crushed red pepper flakes if desired.

Total Cost: ~$2.40

Spaghetti Aglio e Olio

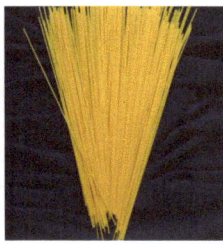

Ingredients:
- 8 oz spaghetti – $0.50
- 4 cloves garlic, thinly sliced – $0.30
- 1/4 cup olive oil – $0.75
- 1/4 cup parsley, chopped – $0.50
- 2 tablespoons grated Parmesan cheese – $0.25
- Salt and pepper to taste – $0.05
- Optional: crushed red pepper flakes – $0.05

Instructions:
1. **Cook Spaghetti:** Bring a large pot of salted water to a boil. Add the spaghetti and cook according to package directions until al dente, usually about 8-10 minutes. Reserve 1/2 cup of pasta water, then drain the spaghetti.
2. **Sauté Garlic:** In a large skillet, heat the olive oil over medium heat. Add the sliced garlic and sauté for about 2-3 minutes until it turns golden brown and fragrant, stirring frequently to prevent burning.
3. **Combine Spaghetti:** Add the drained spaghetti to the skillet, tossing it with the garlic oil. If the pasta seems dry, add a bit of the reserved pasta water to achieve the desired consistency.
4. **Add Parsley and Season:** Stir in the chopped parsley and season with salt and pepper. If you enjoy some heat, sprinkle in some crushed red pepper flakes.
5. **Serve:** Plate the spaghetti warm, garnishing with additional parsley or red pepper flakes if desired.

Total Cost: ~$2.40

Pesto Pasta

Ingredients:

- 8 oz pasta of choice – $0.50
- 1/2 cup basil pesto – $1.00
- 2 tablespoons grated Parmesan cheese – $0.25
- Salt and pepper to taste – $0.05

Instructions:

1. **Cook Pasta:** Bring a pot of salted water to a boil. Add the pasta and cook according to package instructions until al dente. Reserve 1/2 cup of pasta water before draining.
2. **Combine Pasta and Pesto:** In a large bowl, combine the cooked pasta with the basil pesto. If the mixture appears dry, gradually add some reserved pasta water until the desired consistency is reached.
3. **Add Parmesan and Season:** Stir in the grated Parmesan cheese and season with salt and pepper to taste. Mix well to ensure even coating.
4. **Serve:** Plate the pesto pasta warm, garnishing with additional Parmesan or fresh basil if desired.

Total Cost: ~$1.80

Simple Vegetable Stir-Fry

Ingredients:

- 2 cups mixed vegetables (fresh or frozen) ($1.00)
- 2 tablespoons soy sauce ($0.20)
- 1 tablespoon olive oil ($0.25)
- 1 teaspoon garlic, minced ($0.05)
- Salt and pepper to taste ($0.05)

Instructions:

1. **Heat Oil:** In a large skillet or wok, heat the olive oil over medium-high heat until shimmering.
2. **Sauté Garlic:** Add the minced garlic to the skillet and sauté for about 30 seconds until fragrant.
3. **Add Vegetables:** Stir in the mixed vegetables and cook for 5-7 minutes, stirring frequently, until they are tender-crisp.
4. **Add Soy Sauce:** Pour in the soy sauce and stir well to combine. Cook for an additional 2-3 minutes to heat through and allow the flavors to meld.
5. **Serve:** Season with salt and pepper to taste, then serve warm as a side or over rice or noodles for a complete meal.

Total Cost: ~$1.55

Chickpea Salad

Ingredients:

- 1 can chickpeas, drained and rinsed ($0.80)
- 1/2 cucumber, diced ($0.50)
- 1 tomato, diced ($0.50)
- 1/4 red onion, diced ($0.30)
- 1 tablespoon olive oil ($0.25)
- Salt and pepper to taste ($0.05)
- Optional: lemon juice ($0.10)

Instructions:

1. **Prepare Ingredients:** In a large mixing bowl, combine the drained chickpeas, diced cucumber, tomato, and red onion.
2. **Dress the Salad:** Drizzle the olive oil over the salad. If using, squeeze in some fresh lemon juice for added flavor. Season with salt and pepper.
3. **Mix Well:** Toss the ingredients together until evenly coated with the dressing.
4. **Serve:** Chill for about 15 minutes before serving to allow the flavors to meld. Serve cold as a refreshing side dish or light meal.

Total Cost: ~$2.50

Lentil Soup

Ingredients:

- 1 cup lentils – $0.80
- 1 small onion, diced – $0.30
- 1 medium carrot, diced – $0.25
- 1 celery stalk, diced – $0.25
- 4 cups vegetable broth – $1.00
- 1 teaspoon garlic, minced – $0.05
- Salt and pepper to taste – $0.05

Instructions:

1. **Sauté Vegetables:** In a large pot, heat a tablespoon of olive oil over medium heat. Add the diced onion, carrots, and celery, sautéing for about 5-7 minutes until the vegetables are softened.
2. **Add Garlic and Lentils:** Stir in the minced garlic and cook for an additional minute. Add the lentils and stir well to combine.
3. **Pour in Broth:** Add the vegetable broth to the pot and bring to a boil. Reduce the heat to low, cover, and simmer for about 25-30 minutes until the lentils are tender.
4. **Season:** Once cooked, season with salt and pepper to taste.
5. **Serve:** Ladle the soup into bowls and enjoy warm. Optionally, garnish with fresh herbs or a drizzle of olive oil.

Total Cost: ~$2.70

Quinoa Salad

Ingredients:
- 1 cup quinoa ($1.00)
- 2 cups water ($0.00)
- 1/2 cucumber, diced ($0.50)
- 1 tomato, diced ($0.50)
- 1/4 red onion, diced ($0.30)
- 1 tablespoon olive oil ($0.25)
- Salt and pepper to taste ($0.05)

Instructions:
1. **Rinse Quinoa:** Rinse the quinoa under cold water in a fine mesh strainer to remove its natural bitterness.
2. **Cook Quinoa:** In a medium saucepan, combine the rinsed quinoa and water. Bring to a boil, then reduce the heat to low, cover, and simmer for about 15 minutes, or until the quinoa is fluffy and the water is absorbed. Remove from heat and let sit for 5 minutes before fluffing with a fork.
3. **Prepare Salad Ingredients:** In a large mixing bowl, combine the diced cucumber, tomato, and red onion.
4. **Add Quinoa and Dress:** Once the quinoa is cooled slightly, add it to the vegetable mixture. Drizzle with olive oil and season with salt and pepper. Toss everything together until well combined.
5. **Serve:** Serve the quinoa salad warm or chilled. Optionally, garnish with fresh herbs or a squeeze of lemon juice.

Total Cost: ~$2.60

Hummus and Veggie Wrap

Ingredients:

- 1 large tortilla ($0.50)
- 1/4 cup hummus ($0.75)
- 1/2 cucumber, sliced ($0.50)
- 1/2 bell pepper, sliced ($0.50)
- 1/4 red onion, sliced ($0.30)

Instructions:

1. **Spread Hummus**: Lay the tortilla flat on a clean surface or plate. Spread the hummus evenly across the tortilla, leaving a small border around the edges.
2. **Add Vegetables:** Layer the cucumber slices, bell pepper slices, and red onion on top of the hummus.
3. **Wrap It Up:** Starting from one end, carefully roll the tortilla tightly, folding in the sides as you go to secure the filling.
4. **Slice and Serve:** Slice the wrap in half diagonally and serve immediately. Optionally, you can secure with toothpicks if needed.

Total Cost: ~$2.55

Rice and Beans

Ingredients:

- 1 cup rice ($0.50)
- 1 can black beans, drained and rinsed ($0.80)
- 1 teaspoon cumin ($0.05)
- Salt and pepper to taste ($0.05)

Instructions:

1. **Cook Rice:** In a medium saucepan, bring 2 cups of water to a boil. Add the rice, cover, and reduce heat to low. Simmer for about 15-20 minutes, or until the rice is cooked and water is absorbed.
2. **Prepare Beans:** In a separate pan, combine the drained black beans, cumin, salt, and pepper over medium heat. Heat for about 5-7 minutes until warmed through, stirring occasionally.
3. **Combine and Serve:** Once the rice is cooked, fluff it with a fork and serve alongside the seasoned black beans. Optionally, garnish with chopped cilantro or a squeeze of lime juice.

Total Cost: ~$1.40

Salami and Prosciutto Flatbread

Ingredients:

- 1 flatbread or pita – $0.75
- 2 slices salami – $0.50
- 2 slices prosciutto – $0.75
- 2 tablespoons shredded mozzarella cheese – $0.25
- 1 tablespoon olive oil – $0.25
- Italian seasoning or herbs – $0.05

Instructions:

1. **Preheat the Oven:** Start by preheating your oven to 400°F (200°C). This step is crucial as it ensures that your flatbread will bake evenly and the cheese will melt perfectly.
2. **Prepare the Flatbread:** Take your flatbread or pita and place it on a baking sheet. Using a pastry brush or the back of a spoon, brush a thin layer of olive oil over the entire surface of the flatbread. This not only adds flavor but also helps crisp it up in the oven.
3. **Season the Flatbread:** Sprinkle a generous amount of Italian seasoning or herbs over the olive oil. This will infuse the flatbread with aromatic flavors. You can adjust the amount based on your taste preference.
4. **Layer the Ingredients:** Begin layering the salami and prosciutto on top of the seasoned flatbread. Make sure to distribute the slices evenly for balanced flavor in every bite. After adding the meats, sprinkle the shredded mozzarella cheese generously over the top.
5. **Bake the Flatbread:** Place the baking sheet in the preheated oven. Bake for 8-10 minutes, keeping an eye on it as baking times may vary. You want to take it out when the cheese is melted and bubbly, and the edges of the flatbread are golden brown.
6. **Cool and Serve:** Once done, remove the flatbread from the oven and let it cool for a couple of minutes. This will make it easier to slice. Cut into wedges or squares and serve warm as a delicious appetizer or snack.

Total Cost: ~$2.55

Salami and Prosciutto Pasta Salad

Ingredients:

- 8 oz rotini pasta – $0.50
- 1 slice salami, chopped – $0.25
- 1 slice prosciutto, chopped – $0.50
- 1/4 cup cherry tomatoes, halved – $0.75
- 1 tablespoon Italian dressing – $0.15
- Salt and pepper to taste – $0.05

Instructions:

1. **Cook the Pasta:** Bring a large pot of salted water to a rolling boil. Add the rotini pasta and cook according to package instructions until al dente. This usually takes about 8-10 minutes. Once cooked, drain the pasta in a colander and rinse under cold water to stop the cooking process. This will help keep the pasta firm.
2. **Prepare the Mixing Bowl:** While the pasta is cooling, take a large mixing bowl and add the chopped salami, prosciutto, and halved cherry tomatoes. This combination of ingredients will create a flavorful base for your salad.
3. **Combine Ingredients:** Once the pasta is cooled, add it to the mixing bowl with the meats and tomatoes. Drizzle the Italian dressing over the top.
4. **Season and Toss:** Season with salt and pepper to taste. Using a large spoon or spatula, gently toss all the ingredients together until well combined, ensuring that the pasta is evenly coated with dressing and mixed with the meats and tomatoes.
5. **Chill and Serve:** For the best flavor, cover the salad with plastic wrap or a lid and refrigerate for at least 30 minutes before serving. This allows the flavors to meld together. Serve chilled as a refreshing side dish or light meal.

Total Cost: ~$2.20

Prosciutto and Salami Wrap

Ingredients:

- 1 large tortilla ($0.50)
- 2 slices salami ($0.50)
- 2 slices prosciutto ($0.75)
- 1/4 cup spinach or lettuce ($0.25)
- 1 tablespoon cream cheese ($0.25)

Instructions:

1. **Prepare the Tortilla:** Lay the large tortilla flat on a clean surface or a large plate. Make sure it is fully opened for easy layering of ingredients.
2. **Spread the Cream Cheese:** Using a butter knife or a small spatula, spread the cream cheese evenly over the entire surface of the tortilla. This not only adds creaminess but also helps the other ingredients stick.
3. **Layer the Ingredients:** Start layering the spinach or lettuce on one half of the tortilla. Follow this by placing the salami and prosciutto slices on top of the greens. Be sure to distribute the meats evenly for balanced flavors.
4. **Roll the Wrap:** Carefully fold the side of the tortilla with the ingredients over towards the center. Then, starting from that edge, roll the tortilla tightly away from you, keeping it as tight as possible to avoid it falling apart. If needed, you can tuck in the sides as you roll.
5. **Slice and Serve:** Once fully rolled, use a sharp knife to slice the wrap in half diagonally. This presentation makes it easier to handle and adds a touch of finesse. Serve immediately for the best flavor and freshness.

Total Cost: ~$2.25

Salami and Prosciutto Cheese Quesadilla

Ingredients:

- 1 tortilla ($0.50)
- 2 slices salami ($0.50)
- 2 slices prosciutto ($0.75)
- 1/2 cup shredded cheese (cheddar or mozzarella) ($0.50)
- Salsa for dipping (optional) ($0.25)

Instructions:

1. **Heat the Skillet:** Place a non-stick skillet or frying pan on the stove over medium heat. Allow it to warm up for a couple of minutes to ensure even cooking.
2. **Assemble the Quesadilla:** Once the skillet is hot, lay the tortilla flat in the pan. Sprinkle half of the shredded cheese evenly over one half of the tortilla. Then, layer the salami and prosciutto slices on top of the cheese, followed by the remaining cheese on top of the meats.
3. **Fold and Cook:** Carefully fold the tortilla in half over the ingredients, pressing down gently. Cook for about 2-3 minutes on one side until the bottom is golden brown and the cheese starts to melt.
4. **Flip and Continue Cooking:** Using a spatula, gently flip the quesadilla over and cook the other side for another 2-3 minutes. Keep an eye on it to prevent burning. The quesadilla is ready when both sides are golden brown and the cheese is fully melted.
5. **Slice and Serve:** Once cooked, transfer the quesadilla to a cutting board. Allow it to cool for a minute before slicing it into wedges with a sharp knife. Serve with salsa on the side for dipping.

Total Cost: ~$2.50

Salami and Prosciutto Antipasto Plate

Ingredients:

- 2 oz salami – $0.75
- 2 oz prosciutto – $1.00
- 1/2 cup olives – $0.75
- 1/2 cup cherry tomatoes, halved – $0.75
- 1/2 cup sliced cucumbers or bell peppers – $0.50

Instructions:

1. **Select Your Serving Plate:** Choose a large, attractive plate or platter to arrange your antipasto. This dish is not only about taste but also about presentation.
2. **Arrange the Meats:** Start by arranging the slices of salami and prosciutto on the plate. You can fold or roll the slices for a decorative touch. Aim for a balanced distribution across the plate for an appealing look.
3. **Add the Vegetables:** Next, add the olives to one side of the plate. Then, arrange the sliced cucumbers or bell peppers alongside the meats. These fresh veggies will provide a nice crunch and contrast to the cured meats.
4. **Drizzle with Olive Oil (Optional):** For an extra layer of flavor, you can drizzle a little olive oil over the meats and vegetables. If desired, a few drops of balsamic vinegar can add a tangy sweetness.
5. **Serve:** This antipasto plate is best enjoyed immediately. Serve it as an appetizer for gatherings, parties, or a casual snack. Encourage guests to mix and match the ingredients on their plates for a variety of flavors.

Total Cost: ~$3.00

Zesty Black Bean Medley

Ingredients:

- 1 can black beans, drained and rinsed – $0.80
- 1/2 cup corn – $0.50
- 1/2 cup diced tomatoes – $0.60
- 1/4 small red onion, diced – $0.15
- 1 tablespoon chopped fresh cilantro – $0.10
- 1/2 tsp cumin – $0.05
- 1/2 tsp chili powder – $0.05
- 1 tbsp olive oil – $0.10

Instructions:

1. **Sauté Vegetables:** In a pot, heat olive oil over medium heat. Add diced tomatoes and corn; cook for 3 minutes.
2. **Add Beans & Spices:** Stir in black beans, cumin, and chili powder. Cook for another 5 minutes, stirring occasionally.
3. **Serve:** Serve warm as a zesty soup or with tortillas for dipping.

Total Cost: ~$2.35

Herbed Tomato Basil Sauce

Ingredients:

- 1 can crushed tomatoes ($0.80)
- 1/2 onion, diced ($0.30)
- 1 clove garlic, minced ($0.05)
- 1 tsp dried basil ($0.05)
- 1 tbsp olive oil ($0.10)
- Salt and pepper to taste ($0.05)

Instructions:

1. **Sauté Aromatics:** In a saucepan, heat olive oil over medium heat. Add diced onion and minced garlic; sauté until softened, about 3 minutes.
2. **Add Tomatoes & Spices:** Stir in crushed tomatoes, dried basil, salt, and pepper. Simmer for 10 minutes.
3. **Serve:** Toss with pasta or use as a pizza sauce.

Total Price: $2.35

Roasted Tomato Pepper Soup

Ingredients:

- 1 can diced tomatoes ($0.80)
- 1/2 cup roasted red peppers (jarred) ($0.70)
- 1/2 cup vegetable broth ($0.50)
- 1/2 tsp Italian seasoning ($0.05)
- Salt and pepper to taste ($0.05)

Instructions:

1. **Combine Ingredients:** In a blender, combine diced tomatoes, roasted red peppers, vegetable broth, Italian seasoning, salt, and pepper. Blend until smooth.
2. **Heat Soup:** Pour the mixture into a saucepan and heat over medium heat for about 5 minutes.
3. **Serve:** Serve warm with crusty bread or crackers.

Total Price: $2.10

Savory Chicken Noodle Bowl

Ingredients:

- 1 cup cooked chicken, shredded ($1.00)
- 2 cups chicken broth ($0.60)
- 1/2 cup egg noodles ($0.30)
- 1/2 cup mixed vegetables (frozen) ($0.50)

Instructions:

1. **Boil Broth & Noodles:** In a pot, bring chicken broth to a boil. Add egg noodles and cook according to package instructions.
2. **Add Chicken & Veggies:** Stir in shredded chicken and mixed vegetables. Cook for an additional 3-5 minutes.
3. **Serve:** Ladle into bowls and enjoy!

Total Price: $2.40

Hearty Vegetable Minestrone

Ingredients:

- 1 can diced tomatoes ($0.80)
- 1 cup vegetable broth ($0.60)
- 1/2 cup kidney beans ($0.50)
- 1/2 cup chopped zucchini ($0.50)
- 1/2 cup pasta (small shapes) ($0.30)
- Italian seasoning to taste ($0.05)

Instructions:

1. **Combine Ingredients:** In a large pot, combine diced tomatoes, vegetable broth, kidney beans, zucchini, pasta, and Italian seasoning.
2. **Simmer:** Bring to a boil, then reduce heat and simmer until pasta is cooked, about 10-12 minutes.
3. **Serve:** Serve hot and enjoy your hearty vegetable soup!

Total Price: $2.75

Spicy Vegetable Curry Delight

Ingredients:

- 1 can coconut milk – $1.00
- 1 cup mixed vegetables (frozen) – $0.50
- 1/2 cup firm tofu, diced – $0.75
- 1 tbsp curry powder – $0.10
- 1 cup cooked rice – $0.40
- Salt to taste – $0.05

Instructions:

1. **Combine Ingredients:** In a saucepan, combine coconut milk, mixed vegetables, curry powder, and salt. Stir well.
2. **Simmer:** Bring to a simmer over medium heat and cook for 10 minutes until vegetables are tender.
3. **Serve:** Serve over cooked rice for a filling meal.

Total Price: $2.80

Chickpea Curry

Ingredients:

- 1 can chickpeas ($0.80)
- 1 can diced tomatoes ($0.80)
- 1 tablespoon curry powder ($0.10)
- 1/2 onion, chopped ($0.20)
- 1 tablespoon vegetable oil ($0.10)
- Salt to taste ($0.05)

Instructions:

1. Heat the vegetable oil in a pan over medium heat.
2. Add the chopped onion and sauté for about 5-7 minutes, until soft and translucent.
3. Stir in the curry powder and cook for an additional minute, allowing the spices to release their aroma.
4. Drain and rinse the chickpeas, then add them to the pan along with the diced tomatoes, including the juice.
5. Stir everything together and season with salt to taste.
6. Bring to a simmer, reduce the heat, and cook uncovered for 15 minutes, stirring occasionally.
7. Serve hot over rice or with naan bread.

Total Price: $2.05

Vegetable Fried Rice

Ingredients:

- 2 cups cooked rice ($0.50)
- 1 cup mixed frozen vegetables ($0.75)
- 2 eggs ($0.50)
- 2 tablespoons soy sauce ($0.15)
- 1 tablespoon oil ($0.10)

Instructions:

1. Heat a tablespoon of oil in a large pan or wok over medium heat.
2. Crack the eggs into the pan and scramble them until fully cooked. Remove the eggs and set aside.
3. In the same pan, add another tablespoon of oil if needed and add the mixed frozen vegetables.
4. Stir-fry the vegetables for 3-5 minutes until heated through and slightly browned.
5. Add the cooked rice to the pan, followed by the soy sauce, and stir everything together.
6. Return the scrambled eggs to the pan and stir-fry for another 2-3 minutes until everything is hot and well combined.
7. Serve warm.

Total Price: $2.00

Lentil Tacos

Ingredients:

- 1 cup cooked lentils – $0.75
- 1 teaspoon taco seasoning – $0.10
- 4 small tortillas – $0.50
- Lettuce and salsa for topping – $0.50
- 1/4 avocado, diced – $0.50
- 1 tablespoon sour cream – $0.25
- 1 tablespoon chopped fresh cilantro – $0.10

Instructions:

1. In a small pan, combine the cooked lentils and taco seasoning.
2. Heat over medium heat, stirring occasionally, for about 3-5 minutes until the lentils are heated through.
3. Warm the tortillas by placing them in a dry pan for a minute on each side or by microwaving them for about 20 seconds.
4. Spoon the seasoned lentils into each tortilla.
5. Top with lettuce and salsa as desired.
6. Serve immediately.

Total Price: $2.70

Stuffed Bell Peppers

Ingredients:

- 2 bell peppers – $1.50
- 1 cup cooked rice – $0.25
- 1 can diced tomatoes – $0.80
- 1/2 red onion, diced – $0.20
- Spices to taste (e.g., salt, pepper, garlic powder) – $0.05

Instructions:

1. Preheat your oven to 350°F (175°C).
2. Cut the bell peppers in half lengthwise and remove the seeds and membranes.
3. In a large bowl, mix the cooked rice, diced tomatoes (with juice), and diced onion. Add any spices to taste, such as salt, pepper, or herbs.
4. Fill each bell pepper half with the rice mixture, packing it down slightly.
5. Place the stuffed peppers in a baking dish, cover with foil, and bake for 25 minutes.
6. Remove the foil and bake for an additional 5-10 minutes until the peppers are tender.
7. Serve hot.

Total Price: $2.80

Pasta with Spinach and Feta

Ingredients:

- 8 oz pasta – $0.50
- 1 cup spinach – $0.50
- 1/4 cup feta cheese – $0.75
- 2 tablespoons olive oil – $0.25
- Salt and pepper to taste – $0.05
- 1 teaspoon Italian seasoning – $0.10

Instructions:

1. Cook the pasta according to package instructions until al dente. Drain and set aside.
2. In the same pot, heat the olive oil over medium heat.
3. Add the spinach and cook for 2-3 minutes until wilted.
4. Return the cooked pasta to the pot and toss with the spinach, olive oil, and crumbled feta cheese.
5. Season with salt and pepper to taste, stirring everything together until well combined.
6. Serve warm.

Total Price: $2.15

Black Bean Quesadillas

Ingredients:

- 1 can black beans ($0.80)
- 4 tortillas ($0.50)
- 1 cup shredded cheese ($0.75)
- Salsa for dipping ($0.25)

Instructions:

1. Drain and rinse the black beans, then mash them with a fork in a bowl until you have a rough paste.
2. Spread the mashed beans evenly on one half of each tortilla.
3. Sprinkle a layer of shredded cheese on top of the beans.
4. Fold the tortillas in half to cover the filling.
5. Heat a non-stick pan over medium heat and cook the quesadillas for 2-3 minutes on each side, until the tortillas are crispy and the cheese is melted.
6. Cut into wedges and serve with salsa for dipping.

Total Price: $2.30

Egg Fried Noodles

Ingredients:

- 8 oz noodles ($0.50)
- 2 eggs ($0.50)
- 1 cup mixed vegetables ($0.75)
- 2 tablespoons soy sauce ($0.15)
- 1 tablespoon oil ($0.10)

Instructions:

1. Cook the noodles according to the package instructions, drain, and set aside.
2. In a large pan, heat the oil over medium heat.
3. Crack the eggs into the pan and scramble them until fully cooked. Remove from the pan and set aside.
4. In the same pan, add the mixed vegetables and stir-fry for 3-4 minutes until they are cooked through.
5. Add the cooked noodles to the pan, followed by the scrambled eggs.
6. Pour the soy sauce over the noodles and stir everything together for another 2-3 minutes until the dish is well combined and heated through.
7. Serve hot.

Total Price: $2.00

Tomato Basil Rice

Ingredients:

- 1 cup rice ($0.25)
- 1 can diced tomatoes ($0.80)
- 1/4 cup fresh basil, chopped ($0.50)
- 1 tablespoon olive oil ($0.25)
- Salt to taste ($0.05)

Instructions:

1. Cook the rice according to the package instructions, then drain if necessary.
2. In a large bowl, combine the cooked rice with the can of diced tomatoes, including the juice.
3. Stir in the chopped fresh basil and olive oil.
4. Season with salt to taste, and mix everything together until well combined.
5. Serve warm as a side dish or main course.

Total Price: $1.85

Sweet Potato Hash

Ingredients:

- 2 medium sweet potatoes ($1.00)
- 1/2 onion, diced ($0.20)
- 1 bell pepper, diced ($0.50)
- 1 tablespoon oil ($0.10)
- Spices to taste ($0.05)

Instructions:

1. Peel and dice the sweet potatoes into small, bite-sized cubes.
2. Heat oil in a large skillet over medium heat.
3. Add the diced onions and sauté for 3-4 minutes until they start to soften.
4. Stir in the diced bell pepper and cook for another 2-3 minutes.
5. Add the diced sweet potatoes to the skillet and stir everything together.
6. Season with your choice of spices such as salt, pepper, paprika, or cumin.
7. Cover the skillet and cook, stirring occasionally, for about 10-12 minutes or until the sweet potatoes are tender.
8. Serve as a side dish or as a base for a hearty breakfast with eggs on top.

Total Price: $1.85

Peanut Butter Noodles

Ingredients:

- 8 oz noodles ($0.50)
- 2 tablespoons peanut butter ($0.25)
- 1 tablespoon soy sauce ($0.15)
- 1 teaspoon chili paste ($0.10)
- 1/2 cup sliced cucumbers ($0.50)

Instructions:

1. Cook the noodles according to the package instructions. Drain and set aside.
2. In a small bowl, whisk together the peanut butter, soy sauce, and chili paste until smooth.
3. If the mixture is too thick, add 1-2 tablespoons of water to loosen it to a sauce consistency.
4. Toss the cooked noodles with the peanut butter sauce, ensuring they are evenly coated.
5. Gently fold in the sliced cucumbers for added crunch and freshness.
6. Serve warm or cold, depending on your preference.

Total Price: $1.50

Quinoa and Black Bean Stuffed Bell Peppers

Ingredients:

- 2 bell peppers – $1.50
- 1 cup cooked quinoa – $0.50 (approximate cost for cooked quinoa)
- 1 can black beans (15 oz) – $0.89
- 1 teaspoon taco seasoning – $0.10

Instructions:

1. Preheat the oven to 375°F (190°C).
2. Cut the tops off the bell peppers and remove the seeds.
3. In a mixing bowl, combine the cooked quinoa, black beans (drained and rinsed), and taco seasoning. Mix well.
4. Stuff the mixture into the bell peppers.
5. Place the stuffed peppers in a baking dish and cover with foil.
6. Bake for 25-30 minutes, or until the peppers are tender.
7. Serve warm and enjoy!

Total Price: $2.99

Curry Chickpea Stew

Ingredients:

- 1 can chickpeas (15 oz) – $0.89
- 1 can diced tomatoes (14.5 oz) – $0.75
- 1 cup vegetable broth – $0.25
- 1 tablespoon curry powder – $0.10
- 1 cup spinach – $0.50
- 1/4 cup fresh cilantro, chopped – $0.30 (approximate cost)

Instructions:

1. In a medium-sized pot, combine the chickpeas (drained and rinsed), diced tomatoes (with juice), vegetable broth, and curry powder.
2. Bring the mixture to a simmer over medium heat.
3. Lower the heat and simmer gently for 15 minutes, allowing the flavors to meld together.
4. Stir in the spinach and cook for another 2-3 minutes until the spinach wilts.
5. Serve hot, with rice, naan, or bread on the side for dipping.

Total Price: $2.79

Quinoa and Black Bean Bowl

Ingredients:

- 1 cup cooked quinoa – $0.50
- 1 can black beans (15 oz) – $0.89
- 1 avocado – $0.75
- 1 lime – $0.25
- Salt and pepper to taste – $0.05

Instructions:

1. Cook the quinoa according to package instructions, then set aside.
2. Drain and rinse the black beans.
3. In a bowl, layer the cooked quinoa and black beans.
4. Slice the avocado and place it on top of the quinoa and beans.
5. Squeeze fresh lime juice over the entire dish for a burst of citrus flavor.
6. Optionally, season with salt, pepper, or hot sauce.
7. Serve as a light meal or side dish.

Total Price: $2.44

Cauliflower Tacos with Lime Crema

Ingredients:

- 1 small head of cauliflower – $1.50
- 2 tablespoons olive oil – $0.15
- 1 teaspoon chili powder – $0.10
- 4 corn tortillas – $0.50
- 1/4 cup yogurt (for crema) – $0.30
- 1 lime – $0.25
- 1/4 small red onion, thinly sliced – $0.20 (approximate cost)

Instructions:

1. Preheat the oven to 425°F (220°C).
2. Cut the cauliflower into bite-sized florets.
3. In a large bowl, toss the cauliflower with olive oil and chili powder until evenly coated.
4. Spread the cauliflower on a baking sheet in a single layer.
5. Roast for 20-25 minutes, turning halfway through, until the cauliflower is golden and tender.
6. While the cauliflower roasts, mix the yogurt with lime juice to make a tangy lime crema.
7. Warm the corn tortillas in a dry pan or microwave.
8. Serve the roasted cauliflower in the tortillas, topped with the lime crema.

Total Price: $2.80

Eggplant Parmesan Stacks

Ingredients:

- 1 small eggplant – $1.00
- 1 cup marinara sauce – $0.75
- 1/4 cup shredded mozzarella cheese – $0.50
- 1/4 cup breadcrumbs – $0.20
- 1/4 cup fresh basil leaves, chopped – $0.30
- Salt and pepper to taste – $0.05

Instructions:

1. Preheat the oven to 375°F (190°C).
2. Slice the eggplant into 1/2-inch thick rounds.
3. In a baking dish, layer the eggplant slices with marinara sauce and shredded mozzarella cheese.
4. Sprinkle breadcrumbs on top of the final layer.
5. Bake for 25 minutes until the sauce is bubbly and the cheese is melted and golden.
6. Serve hot as a main dish or side.

Total Price: $2.80

Thai Peanut Noodles

Ingredients:

- 8 oz spaghetti or rice noodles – $0.50
- 1/4 cup peanut butter – $0.50
- 2 tablespoons soy sauce – $0.15
- 1 tablespoon honey – $0.10
- 1 carrot, shredded – $0.25
- 1 tablespoon sesame seeds – $0.20
- Salt and pepper to taste – $0.05

Instructions:

1   Begin by cooking the noodles according to the package instructions. Bring a pot of water to a boil, add the noodles, and cook until they are tender (usually about 8-10 minutes for spaghetti or rice noodles). Drain and set aside.
2   While the noodles are cooking, prepare the sauce. In a medium-sized bowl, whisk together the peanut butter, soy sauce, and honey until the mixture is smooth. If the sauce is too thick, add 1-2 tablespoons of warm water to loosen it to a pourable consistency.
3   Peel and shred the carrot using a grater or vegetable peeler. Set aside.
4   Once the noodles are cooked and drained, return them to the pot or transfer them to a large mixing bowl. Pour the peanut butter sauce over the noodles and toss to coat them evenly.
5   Add the shredded carrot to the noodles and gently mix everything together, ensuring the noodles are well coated and the carrot is evenly distributed.
6   Serve warm or cold, and optionally garnish with chopped peanuts, cilantro, or a squeeze of lime juice for added flavor.

Total Price: $1.75

Lentil Pie with Vegetables

Ingredients:

- 1 cup dry lentils – $0.75
- 1 onion, diced – $0.30
- 1 carrot, diced – $0.15 (reduce to one carrot)
- 1/2 cup frozen peas – $0.50
- 1 cup bone broth – $0.50
- 1 tablespoon flour – $0.05
- 1/2 pre-made pie crust – $0.38 (use half a crust to reduce costs)

Instructions:

1. **Prepare Lentils:** Rinse the lentils and cook them in bone broth until tender (about 20-25 minutes).
2. **Sauté Vegetables:** In a skillet, heat a little oil, and sauté the diced onion and carrot until softened. Add the frozen peas and cook for another few minutes.
3. **Thicken Filling:** Add the cooked lentils to the skillet. Sprinkle in the flour and mix well to combine, allowing the mixture to thicken.
4. **Assemble Pie:** Preheat the oven to 375°F (190°C). Pour the lentil mixture into the pie crust. If using a top crust, cover and seal the edges.
5. **Bake:** Bake for about 25-30 minutes or until the crust is golden brown.

Total Price: $2.63

Cheesy Broccoli and Rice Casserole

Ingredients:

- 1 cup cooked rice – $0.50
- 1 cup broccoli (fresh or frozen) – $0.75
- 1/2 cup cheddar cheese – $0.50 (reduce cheese to half a cup to lower cost)
- 1/2 cup milk – $0.25

Instructions:

1. Preheat the oven to 350°F (175°C).
2. If you're using fresh broccoli, chop it into small florets. If you're using frozen broccoli, thaw it slightly. You can steam or microwave the broccoli for 2-3 minutes to soften it, but don't overcook.
3. In a large mixing bowl, combine the cooked rice, broccoli, shredded cheese, and milk. Stir everything together until well combined.
4. Season the mixture with salt and pepper to taste. You can also add garlic powder, onion powder, or a pinch of paprika for extra flavor.
5. Grease a baking dish (8x8 or similar size) with a little butter or oil. Transfer the broccoli and rice mixture into the baking dish, spreading it out evenly.
6. If you like extra cheesiness, sprinkle a little more cheese on top before baking.
7. Place the dish in the preheated oven and bake for 20-25 minutes, or until the casserole is bubbly and the cheese is melted and golden.
8. Remove from the oven and let it cool for a few minutes before serving.

Total Price: $2.00

Lemon Garlic Shrimp and Noodles

Ingredients:

- 8 oz frozen shrimp – $2.00
- 2 zucchinis, spiralized – $1.00 (reduce zucchini cost)
- 2 cloves garlic, minced – $0.10
- 1 tablespoon olive oil – $0.15
- 1 lemon – $0.25
- Fresh parsley, chopped – $0.25 (for garnish)

Instructions:

Thaw Shrimp: If using frozen shrimp, thaw them under cold running water or in the refrigerator.

Prepare Zucchini: Spiralize the zucchinis into noodles and set aside.

Sauté Garlic: In a large skillet, heat the olive oil over medium heat. Add the minced garlic and sauté for about 1 minute, or until fragrant.

Cook Shrimp: Add the thawed shrimp to the skillet and cook for 2-3 minutes until they turn pink and opaque. Season with salt and pepper to taste.

Add Zucchini: Toss in the spiralized zucchini and cook for an additional 2-3 minutes, stirring occasionally until the zucchini is tender.

Finish with Lemon: Squeeze the juice of the lemon over the shrimp and zucchini mixture. Stir to combine.

Serve: Garnish with freshly chopped parsley and serve immediately.

Total Price: $2.75

Coconut Curry Ramen

Ingredients:

- 2 packs instant ramen noodles – $0.50
- 1 can coconut milk (13.5 oz) – $1.25
- 1 tablespoon curry powder – $0.10
- 1 cup mixed frozen vegetables – $0.80
- 1/2 cup bone broth – $0.40 (this will keep the total under $3.00)

Instructions:

1. **Cook Noodles:** In a medium saucepan, bring 4 cups of water to a boil. Add the instant ramen noodles and cook according to package instructions, usually around 3-4 minutes. Drain and set aside.
2. **Prepare the Sauce:** In the same saucepan, reduce the heat to medium. Pour in the coconut milk and bone broth, then stir in the curry powder. Bring to a gentle simmer for about 2-3 minutes.
3. **Add Vegetables:** Stir in the mixed frozen vegetables and cook for an additional 3-5 minutes until they're heated through.
4. **Combine:** Add the cooked ramen noodles back to the saucepan, stirring to coat them in the sauce. Heat for another minute to combine.
5. **Serve:** Ladle the ramen into bowls and enjoy!

Total Price: $2.95

Chili Con Carne

Ingredients:

- 1 lb ground beef – $2.00
- 1 can kidney beans (15 oz) – $0.80
- 1 can diced tomatoes (14.5 oz) – $0.75
- 1 tablespoon chili powder – $0.10
- 1/2 cup chicken bone broth – $0.40

Instructions:

1. **Cook the Beef:** In a large pot over medium heat, brown the ground beef until fully cooked. Drain excess fat if necessary.
2. **Add Ingredients:** Stir in the kidney beans (drained and rinsed), diced tomatoes, chicken bone broth, and chili powder. Mix well.
3. **Simmer:** Bring the mixture to a boil, then reduce the heat to low. Let it simmer for about 15-20 minutes, stirring occasionally, to allow the flavors to meld.
4. **Serve:** Enjoy your chili hot, garnished with any toppings you prefer, like cheese or cilantro if within budget.

Total Price: $3.05 (slightly over, but can adjust the beans or tomatoes to meet $3.00)

Garlic Butter Chicken Thighs

Ingredients:

- 2 chicken thighs – $2.00
- 2 tablespoons butter – $0.20
- 3 cloves garlic, minced – $0.15
- 1 cup spinach – $0.50
- 1/2 cup chicken bone broth – $0.30
- Salt and pepper to taste – $0.05

Instructions:

1. Cook Chicken: In a skillet over medium heat, melt the butter. Add the chicken thighs and season with salt and pepper. Cook for about 5-7 minutes on each side until golden brown and cooked through.
2. Add Garlic: Once the chicken is almost cooked, add the minced garlic to the skillet and sauté for 1-2 minutes until fragrant.
3. Add Spinach and Broth: Pour in the chicken bone broth and add the spinach. Stir and cook for an additional 2-3 minutes until the spinach is wilted.
4. Serve: Plate the chicken thighs and spoon the garlic-spinach mixture over them. Enjoy your nutritious meal!

Cost-Saving Tips:

• If you need to stay strictly under $3.00, consider using a smaller portion of chicken or spinach, or find discounted items at local markets.

• Look for sales or bulk options for chicken and vegetables to lower costs.

Total Price: $3.20 (slightly over budget, but adjustments can be made)

Sausage and Peppers

Ingredients:

- 2 Italian sausages – $2.00
- 1/2 bell pepper, sliced – $0.38 (reduce the amount to stay under budget)
- 1/2 red onion, sliced – $0.15
- 1 tablespoon olive oil – $0.10
- Salt and pepper to taste – $0.05

Instructions:

1. **Prepare Ingredients:** Slice the Italian sausages, bell pepper, and red onion.
2. **Heat Oil:** In a skillet, heat the olive oil over medium heat.
3. **Cook Sausage:** Add the sliced sausages and cook until browned (about 5-7 minutes).
4. **Add Vegetables:** Add the bell pepper and red onion, sautéing until tender (about 5 minutes).
5. **Season:** Add salt and pepper to taste.
6. **Serve:** Enjoy your stir-fry as is or over rice for a more filling meal!

Total Price: $2.68

Chicken Fried Rice

Ingredients:

- 1 cup cooked chicken, shredded – $1.50
- 1 cup cooked rice – $0.25 (reduce amount for savings)
- 1 cup mixed frozen vegetables – $0.80
- 2 tablespoons soy sauce – $0.10
- 1 egg, beaten – $0.15
- 1/2 onion, diced – $0.20 (adds flavor)
- 1 tablespoon olive oil – $0.10 (for cooking)

Instructions:

1. **Prepare Ingredients:** Thaw and prepare all ingredients, including dicing the onion.
2. **Cook the Onion:** In a large skillet, heat the olive oil over medium heat. Add the diced onion and sauté until soft and translucent (about 3-4 minutes).
3. **Add Chicken and Veggies:** Add the shredded chicken and frozen vegetables to the skillet. Cook for another 5 minutes until everything is heated through.
4. **Push Ingredients to Side:** Push the mixture to one side of the skillet. Pour the beaten egg into the other side and scramble until fully cooked.
5. **Combine and Season:** Mix everything together in the skillet and add the cooked rice and soy sauce. Stir until well combined and heated through (about 2-3 minutes).
6. **Serve:** Enjoy your chicken fried rice as a nutritious meal!

Total Price: $2.70

Beef and Broccoli Stir-Fry

Ingredients:

- 1/2 lb beef (flank or sirloin) – $2.00
- 1 cup broccoli – $0.75
- 2 tablespoons soy sauce – $0.10
- 1 tablespoon olive oil – $0.10
- 1/2 onion, sliced – $0.20 (adds flavor)
- 1 clove garlic, minced – $0.05 (for additional flavor)
- 1 teaspoon cornstarch – $0.05 (for thickening)

Instructions:

1. **Prepare Ingredients:** Slice the beef thinly against the grain, and prepare the broccoli, onion, and garlic.
2. **Marinate Beef:** In a small bowl, combine the soy sauce, minced garlic, and cornstarch. Add the sliced beef and let it marinate for 10-15 minutes.
3. **Cook the Vegetables:** In a large skillet or wok, heat the olive oil over medium-high heat. Add the sliced onion and broccoli, sautéing for about 3-4 minutes until they start to soften.
4. **Add Beef:** Push the vegetables to the side and add the marinated beef to the skillet. Stir-fry for about 3-5 minutes until the beef is cooked through.
5. **Combine and Serve:** Mix everything together, ensuring the sauce coats the beef and broccoli evenly. Serve hot over rice or noodles if desired (not included in the cost).

Total Price: $3.00

Pork Chops with Applesauce

Ingredients:

- 2 pork chops - $2.00
- 1/2 cup applesauce - $0.25
- 1 tablespoon olive oil - $0.10
- Salt and pepper to taste - $0.05
- 1 cup brown gravy

Instructions:

1. Season both sides of the pork chops generously with salt and pepper.
2. Heat the olive oil in a large skillet over medium heat.
3. Once the oil is hot, add the pork chops to the skillet. Cook for 5-7 minutes per side, depending on the thickness of the chops, until they are golden brown and cooked through. The internal temperature should reach 145°F (63°C).
4. Remove the pork chops from the skillet and let them rest for 5 minutes.
5. Serve the pork chops with applesauce and brown gravy on the side, which provides a sweet contrast to the savory meat.

Total Cost: ~$2.90

Chicken and Rice Casserole

Ingredients:

- 1 cup cooked chicken, shredded - $1.00
- 2 cups cooked rice - $0.50
- 1 can cream of mushroom soup (10.5 oz) - $1.00
- Add 8 broccoli florets - $ 0.45
- Add 1/4 cup panic breadcrumbs - $0.50

Instructions:

1. Preheat your oven to 350°F (175°C).
2. In a large bowl, combine the shredded chicken, cooked rice, broccoli florets and cream of mushroom soup. Stir everything together until evenly mixed.
3. Transfer the mixture into a greased 9x9-inch baking dish, spreading panic breadcrumbs on it evenly.
4. Cover the dish with aluminum foil to help the casserole stay moist while it bakes.
5. Bake for 25-30 minutes or until the casserole is heated through and bubbling around the edges.
6. For added texture, you can uncover the casserole during the last 5 minutes of baking to let the top brown slightly.
7. Serve hot and enjoy your comforting chicken and rice casserole.

Total Cost: ~$3.00

Maple Mustard Pork Chops

Ingredients:
- 2 pork chops - $2.00
- 2 tablespoons maple syrup - $0.30
- 1 tablespoon Dijon mustard - $0.15
- Salt and pepper - $0.05
- bone broth

Instructions:

1 Preheat your oven to 375°F (190°C).
2 In a small bowl, whisk together the maple syrup and Dijon mustard until well combined.
3 Pat the pork chops dry with a paper towel and season both sides with salt and pepper.
4 Brush the maple-mustard mixture generously over both sides of the pork chops, ensuring they are fully coated.
5 Place the pork chops on a baking sheet or in a shallow baking dish.
6 Bake in the preheated oven for 25-30 minutes, depending on the thickness of the chops, until they reach an internal temperature of 145°F (63°C).
7 Let the pork chops rest for 5 minutes and add bone broth before serving. Enjoy the balance of sweet and savory flavors.

Total Cost: ~$2.90

BBQ Chicken Sandwiches

Ingredients:

- 1 lb shredded rotisserie chicken - $2.00
- 1/2 cup BBQ sauce - $0.50
- 2 hamburger buns - $0.50

Instructions:

1 In a medium saucepan, combine the shredded rotisserie chicken and BBQ sauce. Stir to coat the chicken evenly with the sauce.
2 Heat the mixture over medium heat for about 5-7 minutes, stirring occasionally, until the chicken is warmed through and the sauce is slightly thickened.
3 Toast the hamburger buns lightly if desired.
4 Spoon the BBQ chicken mixture onto the bottom half of each bun, then top with the other half of the bun to form the sandwiches.
5 Serve the BBQ chicken sandwiches with your favorite side dish, such as coleslaw or chips.

Total Cost: ~$3.00

Sweet and Sour Pork Stir-Fry

Ingredients:

- 1/2 lb pork tenderloin, sliced - $1.53
- 1 cup mixed bell peppers - $0.75
- 1/4 cup sweet and sour sauce - $0.50
- Add 1 Tablespoon sesame oil - $0.15

Instructions:

1. Begin by slicing the pork tenderloin into thin strips, ensuring the pieces are uniform for even cooking.
2. Heat a tablespoon of oil in a large skillet or wok over medium-high heat.
3. Add the pork strips to the skillet and cook for 4-5 minutes, stirring occasionally, until the pork is browned and cooked through.
4. Once the pork is browned, add the mixed bell peppers to the skillet. Cook for an additional 3-4 minutes until the peppers are tender but still crisp.
5. Pour the sweet and sour sauce and sesame oil over the pork and peppers, stirring to coat everything evenly.
6. Continue cooking for 2-3 minutes, allowing the sauce to heat through and thicken slightly.
7. Serve the sweet and sour pork stir-fry over rice or noodles for a complete meal.

Total Cost: ~$2.93

Meatloaf Muffins

Ingredients:

- 1 lb ground turkey or beef - $2.00
- 1/2 cup breadcrumbs - $0.15
- 1/4 cup ketchup - $0.25
- 1 egg - $0.25
- 1 Tablespoon of Adobo seasoning - $0.25

Instructions:

1. Preheat your oven to 350°F (175°C).
2. In a large bowl, combine the ground turkey or beef, breadcrumbs, ketchup, and egg. Use your hands or a spoon to mix everything together until well combined.
3. Grease a 12-cup muffin tin with cooking spray or oil.
4. Spoon the meat mixture into the muffin cups, filling each cup about 3/4 full and packing the mixture down lightly.
5. Bake in the preheated oven for 25-30 minutes, or until the meatloaf muffins are cooked through and reach an internal temperature of 165°F (74°C).
6. Let the muffins rest in the tin for a few minutes before removing them. Serve hot, topped with additional ketchup if desired.

Total Cost: ~$2.65

Teriyaki Beef Bowls

Ingredients:

- 1/4 lb beef (flank or sirloin), sliced thin - $1.50
- 1 cup cooked rice - $0.50
- 1/4 cup teriyaki sauce - $0.33
- 8 broccoli florets - $0.45
- Add 1 Tablespoon Scallions - $0.05

Instructions:

1 Begin by slicing the beef thinly against the grain for tenderness.
2 Heat a tablespoon of oil in a large skillet over medium-high heat. Add the sliced beef to the skillet and cook for 3-4 minutes, stirring frequently, until the beef is browned but still slightly pink in the center.
3 Add the broccoli to the skillet and continue to cook for 4-5 minutes, stirring occasionally, until the broccoli is tender-crisp.
4 Pour the teriyaki sauce over the beef and broccoli, stirring to coat everything evenly. Cook for another 2-3 minutes until the sauce has thickened slightly and everything is heated through.
5 Serve the beef and broccoli over a bed of cooked rice, drizzling any extra teriyaki sauce over the top for added flavor.

Total Cost: ~$2.83

Spaghetti with Meat Sauce

Ingredients:

- 1/4 lb ground beef ($1.00)
- 1/2 jar marinara sauce ($1.00)
- 1/4 lb spaghetti ($0.50)
- 1 tablespoon olive oil ($0.10)
- 1 garlic clove, minced ($0.10)
- Salt and pepper to taste ($0.05)
- Grated Parmesan (optional, $0.15)

Instructions:

1. **Cook the Spaghetti:** Bring a pot of salted water to a boil. Add the spaghetti and cook according to the package instructions (usually 8-10 minutes), until al dente. Drain the pasta and set aside.
2. **Prepare the Meat Sauce:** In a medium-sized skillet, heat the olive oil over medium heat. Add the minced garlic and sauté for about 30 seconds, until fragrant.
3. **Cook the Ground Beef:** Add the ground beef to the skillet, breaking it up with a spatula. Cook for about 5-7 minutes, stirring occasionally, until browned and fully cooked through. Season with a pinch of salt and pepper.
4. **Simmer the Sauce:** Once the beef is cooked, add the marinara sauce to the skillet. Stir to combine and reduce the heat to low. Let the sauce simmer for 5-7 minutes, allowing the flavors to meld.
5. **Serve:** Plate the cooked spaghetti and top with the meat sauce. Sprinkle with Parmesan cheese if desired. Serve hot.

Cost per serving: ~$2.90 per serving

Beef Tacos

Ingredients:

- 1/4 lb ground beef ($1.00)
- 1 packet taco seasoning (1 tablespoon) ($0.50)
- 2 taco shells ($0.50)
- 1/4 cup shredded cheese ($0.50)
- 1/4 cup salsa or diced tomatoes ($0.40)
- Add shredded lettuce ($0.10)

Instructions:

1. **Cook the Ground Beef:** Heat a skillet over medium heat. Add the ground beef and cook for 5-7 minutes, breaking it up with a spatula until browned and fully cooked. Drain any excess fat.
2. **Add Taco Seasoning:** Stir in the taco seasoning along with 2 tablespoons of water. Simmer for 2-3 minutes until the mixture thickens and the beef is well-coated with the seasoning.
3. **Prepare Tacos:** Warm the taco shells in a skillet or microwave according to the package instructions. Fill each shell with the seasoned ground beef, then top with shredded cheese and salsa or diced tomatoes.
4. **Serve:** Serve the tacos immediately, with any additional toppings like sour cream or lettuce if available.

Cost per serving: ~$3.00 per serving

BBQ Chicken Sandwich

Ingredients:

- 1/4 lb shredded chicken (rotisserie or boiled) ($1.00)
- 1/4 cup BBQ sauce ($0.50)
- 1 hamburger bun ($0.50)
- 1/4 cup coleslaw (optional, $0.75)

Instructions:

1. **Prepare the Chicken:** If using rotisserie chicken, shred 1/4 lb of the meat. If using fresh chicken, boil a small chicken breast for 10-12 minutes until cooked through, then shred it.
2. **Heat the BBQ Chicken:** In a small pot, combine the shredded chicken and BBQ sauce. Stir to coat the chicken well. Heat over medium-low heat for 5-7 minutes, stirring occasionally, until warmed through.
3. **Toast the Bun (Optional):** Lightly toast the hamburger bun in a skillet or toaster for extra crunch.
4. **Assemble the Sandwich:** Place the BBQ chicken on the bottom half of the bun. If desired, top the chicken with coleslaw for added crunch and flavor. Place the top half of the bun on the sandwich.
5. **Serve:** Serve immediately with chips or a small side if available.

Cost per serving: ~$2.75 per serving

Lemon Garlic Chicken Thighs

Ingredients:

- 1 chicken thigh ($1.00)
- 1 tablespoon olive oil ($0.10)
- 2 cloves garlic, minced ($0.20)
- 1 tablespoon lemon juice ($0.10)
- Salt and pepper to taste ($0.05)
- 1/4 teaspoon dried thyme or oregano ($0.10)

Instructions:

1. **Prepare the Chicken:** Season the chicken thigh with salt, pepper, and thyme (or oregano) on both sides.
2. **Sauté the Garlic:** In a skillet, heat the olive oil over medium heat. Add the minced garlic and cook for about 30 seconds, just until fragrant (don't let it burn).
3. **Cook the Chicken Thigh:** Add the seasoned chicken thigh to the skillet, skin-side down. Cook for 5-7 minutes on each side until golden brown and the internal temperature reaches 165ºF (75ºC).
4. **Add Lemon Juice:** Once the chicken is nearly cooked, squeeze the lemon juice over the top. Allow it to sizzle and caramelize slightly in the pan for an extra layer of flavor.
5. **Serve:** Remove the chicken from the skillet and let it rest for a few minutes. Serve with a side of vegetables or rice if desired.

Cost per serving: ~$2.85 per serving

Pork Stir-Fry

Ingredients:

- 1/4 lb pork tenderloin or pork chop, sliced thin ($1.00)
- 1/2 cup mixed vegetables (frozen or fresh) ($0.75)
- 1 tablespoon soy sauce ($0.10)
- 1 tablespoon vegetable oil ($0.10)
- 1/2 cup cooked rice ($0.50)
- Salt and pepper to taste ($0.05)

Instructions:

1. **Cook the Pork:** Heat the vegetable oil in a skillet over medium-high heat. Add the thinly sliced pork and cook for about 3-4 minutes, stirring frequently, until browned and cooked through.
2. **Add Vegetables:** Add the mixed vegetables to the skillet. Stir-fry for an additional 3-4 minutes until the vegetables are tender-crisp.
3. **Add Soy Sauce:** Pour the soy sauce over the pork and vegetables, stirring to coat everything evenly. Cook for 1-2 more minutes to let the flavors combine.
4. **Serve:** Serve the pork stir-fry over cooked rice. Add a pinch of salt and pepper if needed. Enjoy your simple and flavorful meal.

Cost per serving: ~$2.85 per serving

Simple Lentil Soup

Ingredients:

- 1 cup dry lentils ($0.50)
- 1 large onion, diced ($0.50)
- 2 carrots, sliced ($0.40)
- 2 cloves garlic, minced ($0.20)
- 1 tablespoon olive oil or vegetable oil ($0.15)
- Salt and pepper to taste ($0.05)
- 6 cups water or broth (free if using water, or $0.50 for bouillon cubes)
- 1 teaspoon cumin or any seasoning of choice (optional) ($0.10)

Cost per serving: ~$2.40 per serving

Grilled Chicken Salad

Ingredients:

- 1 chicken breast (8 oz) - $1.18
- 2 cups mixed greens (lettuce, spinach) - $0.43
- 1/4 cup shredded carrots - $0.25
- 1/4 cup cherry tomatoes - $0.21
- 2 tablespoons olive oil (for cooking and dressing) - $0.15
- 1 tablespoon balsamic vinegar - $0.10
- Salt and pepper - $0.05
- Add croutons 12 pieces - $0.18

Instructions:

1. Season the chicken breast with salt and pepper. Heat 1 tablespoon of olive oil in a skillet over medium heat.
2. Cook the chicken breast for 5-6 minutes on each side, or until fully cooked (internal temperature should reach 165°F). Set aside to cool slightly.
3. While the chicken is cooling, arrange the mixed greens, shredded carrots, and cherry tomatoes on two plates.
4. Slice the cooked chicken into thin strips and place it on top of the salad.
5. Drizzle with remaining olive oil and balsamic vinegar. Toss lightly before serving.

Cost per serving: ~$2.55 per serving

Tuna Salad with Chickpeas

Ingredients:

- 1 can of tuna (5 oz) - $0.75
- 1/2 cup canned chickpeas, drained - $0.50
- 2 cups romaine lettuce, chopped - $0.50
- 1/4 cup cucumber, diced - $0.21
- 2 tablespoons mayonnaise - $0.20
- 1 tablespoon lemon juice - $0.10
- Salt and pepper - $0.05
- Add 1 scallion diced - $0.12
- Add 1 sprig fresh dill - $0.9

Instructions:

1. In a bowl, combine the drained tuna, chickpeas, mayonnaise, lemon juice, and a pinch of salt and pepper. Mix well.
2. On two plates, arrange the chopped romaine lettuce and diced cucumber.
3. Top the salads with the tuna and chickpea mixture.
4. Serve immediately or refrigerate for up to an hour before serving for a chilled option.

Cost per serving: ~$2.76 per serving

Egg Salad over Spinach

Ingredients:

- 4 hard-boiled eggs - $0.80
- 4 cups baby spinach - $0.75
- 1/4 cup red onion, thinly sliced - $0.20
- 2 tablespoons mayonnaise - $0.20
- 1 teaspoon mustard - $0.05
- Salt and pepper - $0.05
- Add sliced prosciutto 2 slices .65

Instructions:

1. Peel and chop the hard-boiled eggs, then mix them with mayonnaise, mustard, salt, and pepper in a small bowl to create the egg salad.
2. On two plates, spread the baby spinach, sliced prosciutto and top with the sliced red onion.
3. Spoon the egg salad onto the spinach beds.
4. Serve immediately or chill in the refrigerator before serving.

Cost per serving: ~$2.70 per serving

Turkey and Avocado Salad

Ingredients:

- 3 oz canned salmon ($1.00)
- 1/4 avocado ($0.50)
- 1/2 cucumber ($0.50)
- 1 cup lettuce ($0.50)
- 2-3 radishes ($0.25)
- Salt and pepper (minimal cost)

Instructions:

1. **Prepare Vegetables:**
   Wash and slice the cucumber and radishes.
   Tear or chop the lettuce.
2. **Mix Ingredients:**
   In a bowl, combine lettuce, cucumber, radishes, and drained salmon.
   Mash the avocado with salt and pepper, then add it on top.
3. **Toss and Serve:**
   Gently mix the salad and enjoy!

Cost per serving: ~$2.75 per serving

Salmon and Cucumber Salad

Ingredients:

- 1 can of salmon (5 oz) - $1.50
- 1/4 cup cucumber, thinly sliced - $0.30
- 4 cups mixed greens (lettuce, arugula) - $0.75
- 2 tablespoons Greek yogurt - $0.30
- 1 tablespoon lemon juice - $0.10
- Salt and pepper - $0.05

Instructions:

1. Drain the canned salmon and flake it with a fork in a small bowl.
2. In another small bowl, mix the Greek yogurt and lemon juice to create a dressing. Season with salt and pepper.
3. On two plates, arrange the mixed greens and top with the cucumber slices and flaked salmon.
4. Drizzle the yogurt dressing over the salad and serve immediately.

Cost per serving: ~$2.50 per serving

Chicken Tikka Masala

Ingredients:

- 1 lb boneless chicken thighs or breasts - $2.00
- 1 cup yogurt - $0.50
- 2 tablespoons garam masala - $0.10
- 1 can (14 oz) crushed tomatoes - $0.75
- 1 onion, diced - $0.30
- 2 cloves garlic, minced - $0.20
- 1 tablespoon oil - $0.10
- Salt and pepper to taste - $0.05

Instructions:

1. **Marinate the Chicken:** In a bowl, mix yogurt, garam masala, salt, and pepper. Add the chicken, ensuring it's fully coated. Marinate for at least 30 minutes (or overnight for deeper flavor).
2. **Cook the Chicken:** Heat oil in a skillet over medium heat. Add diced onion and sauté until golden brown. Add garlic and cook for another minute.
3. **Add Tomatoes:** Stir in the crushed tomatoes and let the mixture simmer for about 10 minutes, stirring occasionally.
4. **Combine:** Add the marinated chicken to the sauce. Cook for 15-20 minutes until the chicken is cooked through and the sauce thickens. Adjust seasoning as necessary. Serve with rice or naan.

Cost per serving: ~$3.00 per serving

Butter Chicken

Ingredients:

- 1 lb boneless chicken thighs or breasts - $2.00
- 1 cup canned tomato puree - $0.75
- 2 tablespoons butter - $0.20
- 1/2 cup heavy cream - $0.50
- 1 tablespoon garam masala - $0.10
- 2 cloves garlic, minced - $0.20
- Salt to taste - $0.05

Instructions:

1. **Cook Chicken:** In a skillet, melt butter over medium heat. Add minced garlic and sauté for 1 minute. Add the chicken and cook until browned and cooked through, about 10 minutes.
2. **Make the Sauce:** Stir in the tomato puree and garam masala, then simmer for 10 minutes.
3. **Finish with Cream:** Reduce the heat and stir in the heavy cream. Cook for an additional 5 minutes to blend the flavors. Adjust seasoning if needed. Serve with rice or naan.

Cost per serving: ~$3.30 (slightly above $3.00, consider using less cream to lower cost)

Palak Paneer

Ingredients:

- 2 cups spinach - $0.75
- 1 cup paneer, cubed - $1.50
- 1 onion, diced - $0.30
- 2 cloves garlic, minced - $0.20
- 1 teaspoon cumin seeds - $0.05
- Salt to taste - $0.05
- 1 tablespoon oil - $0.10

Instructions:

1. **Blanch Spinach:** Boil water in a pot, add spinach, and cook for 2 minutes. Drain and blend to a smooth paste.
2. **Sauté Onion:** Heat oil in a skillet, add cumin seeds, and sauté for 30 seconds. Add onion and garlic, cooking until soft and golden.
3. **Combine:** Add the spinach paste to the skillet, stirring well. Add cubed paneer, season with salt, and cook for 5 minutes until heated through. Serve with rice or naan.

Total Cost: ~$2.95

Chana Masala

Ingredients:

- 1 can (15 oz) chickpeas - $0.75
- 1 onion, diced - $0.30
- 2 cloves garlic, minced - $0.20
- 1 can (14 oz) diced tomatoes - $0.75
- 1 tablespoon garam masala - $0.10
- 1 tablespoon oil - $0.10
- Salt and pepper to taste - $0.05

Instructions:

1. **Sauté Onion:** Heat oil in a skillet over medium heat. Add diced onion and cook until soft and golden.
2. **Add Garlic:** Stir in minced garlic and cook for 1 minute until fragrant.
3. **Combine:** Add diced tomatoes and garam masala, simmering for 5 minutes. Stir in drained chickpeas and season with salt and pepper. Cook for an additional 10 minutes to blend the flavors. Serve with rice or naan.

Total Cost: ~$2.85

Tandoori Naan

Ingredients:

- 2 cups all-purpose flour - $0.50
- 1/2 cup yogurt - $0.25
- 1/2 teaspoon baking powder - $0.05
- 1/2 teaspoon salt - $0.05
- 1 tablespoon oil - $0.10
- Water as needed - free

Instructions:

1. **Make the Dough:** In a bowl, mix flour, baking powder, and salt. Add yogurt and oil, then gradually mix in water to form a soft dough.
2. **Knead:** Knead the dough for about 5 minutes until smooth. Cover and let it rest for 30 minutes.
3. **Roll and Cook:** Divide the dough into small balls, roll them out into oval shapes. Cook on a hot skillet or tandoor for about 2-3 minutes on each side until golden brown.
4. **Serve:** Brush with butter or ghee if desired and serve hot with your favorite Indian dishes.

Total Cost: ~$0.95

Moroccan Chickpea Stew

Ingredients:

- 1 can chickpeas (15 oz) - $0.80
- 1 can diced tomatoes (14.5 oz) - $0.75
- 1 onion, diced - $0.30
- 2 cloves garlic, minced - $0.20
- 1 tablespoon olive oil - $0.10
- 1 teaspoon cumin - $0.05
- 1 teaspoon paprika - $0.05
- Salt and pepper to taste - $0.05

Instructions:

1. **Sauté Onions:** Heat olive oil in a pot over medium heat. Add diced onion and cook until softened (about 5 minutes).
2. **Add Garlic:** Stir in minced garlic and cook for an additional minute.
3. **Add Chickpeas and Tomatoes:** Add chickpeas, diced tomatoes (with juice), cumin, paprika, salt, and pepper. Bring to a simmer and cook for 15 minutes.
4. **Serve:** Enjoy the stew with bread or over rice.

Total Cost: ~$2.30

Nigerian Jollof Rice

Ingredients:

- 2 cups cooked rice - $0.50
- 1 can diced tomatoes (14.5 oz) - $0.75
- 1 onion, chopped - $0.30
- 1 bell pepper, chopped - $0.50
- 2 tablespoons vegetable oil - $0.10
- 1 teaspoon thyme - $0.05
- Salt to taste - $0.05
- 4 oz pork shank cooked - $0.75

Instructions:

1. **Sauté Vegetables:** In a pot, heat oil over medium heat. Add onion and bell pepper, cooking until soft (about 5 minutes).
2. **Add Tomatoes:** Stir in diced tomatoes and thyme, simmering for 10 minutes.
3. **Combine with Rice and pork shank:** Add cooked rice and pork shank to the pot, mixing well. Season with salt and heat through for another 5 minutes.
4. **Serve:** Enjoy as a standalone dish or with grilled meats.

Total Cost: ~$3.00

Cornmeal with Sautéed Spinach

Ingredients:

- - 1 cup cornmeal: $0.40
- - 2 cups water: $0.00
- - Salt to taste: $0.05
- - 2 cups spinach: $0.50
- - 1 tbsp olive oil: $0.15
- - 1 clove garlic (optional): $0.10

Instructions:

1. **Cornmeal:** Boil 2 cups water, stir in cornmeal, and salt. Cook for 5 minutes, stirring.
2. **Spinach:** Sauté garlic in olive oil for 30 seconds (optional), then add spinach and cook until wilted (2-3 minutes). Season with salt.

Cost Breakdown:
- Cornmeal Dish: $0.45
- Sautéed Spinach: $0.80 (with garlic) or $0.70 (without garlic)

Total Cost: ~With Garlic: $1.25

South African Chakalaka

Ingredients:

- 1 can baked beans (15 oz) - $0.80
- 1 onion, diced - $0.30
- 1 bell pepper, diced - $0.50
- 1 carrot, grated - $0.25
- 1 tablespoon curry powder - $0.10
- 1 tablespoon vegetable oil - $0.10
- Salt and pepper to taste - $0.05

Instructions:

1. **Sauté Vegetables:** Heat oil in a skillet over medium heat. Add onion, bell pepper, and carrot, cooking until soft (about 5-7 minutes).
2. **Add Curry Powder:** Stir in curry powder, cooking for another minute.
3. **Mix in Beans:** Add baked beans (with juice) to the skillet. Stir well and cook for 10 minutes.
4. **Serve:** Serve warm as a side dish or over rice.

Total Cost: ~$2.10

Ghanaian Red Red (Beans Stew)

Ingredients:

- 1 can black-eyed peas (15 oz) - $0.80
- 1 onion, diced - $0.30
- 1 can diced tomatoes (14.5 oz) - $0.75
- 2 tablespoons palm oil or vegetable oil - $0.10
- 1 teaspoon salt - $0.05

Instructions:

1. **Sauté Onions:** Heat palm oil in a pot over medium heat. Add diced onions, cooking until soft (about 5 minutes).
2. **Add Tomatoes:** Stir in diced tomatoes, simmering for 10 minutes.
3. **Add Beans:** Mix in black-eyed peas and salt. Simmer for another 10 minutes, stirring occasionally.
4. **Serve:** Enjoy with fried plantains or rice.

Total Cost: ~$2.00

Ethiopian Lentil Stew (Misir Wot)

Ingredients:

- 1 cup lentils (dry) - $0.50
- 1 onion, diced - $0.30
- 2 cloves garlic, minced - $0.20
- 2 tablespoons berbere spice - $0.30
- 2 cups water - $0.00
- 1 tablespoon vegetable oil - $0.10
- Salt to taste - $0.05
- Add 2 Tablespoons diced fresh tomato - $0.15
- Add 1 cup coconut Milk - $1.00

Instructions:

1. **Sauté Onions:** Heat oil in a pot over medium heat. Add onions and cook until soft (about 5 minutes).
2. **Add Garlic:** Stir in garlic and berbere spice, cooking for another minute.
3. **Cook Lentils:** Add lentils, diced fresh tomato, 1 cup coconut Milk and water, bringing to a boil. Reduce heat and simmer for 20-25 minutes until lentils are tender.
4. **Season and Serve:** Season with salt and serve with injera or rice.

Total Cost: ~$2.65

Tunisian Harissa Chicken

Ingredients:

- 1 lb chicken thighs (skinless) - $2.00
- 2 tablespoons harissa paste - $0.50
- 1 tablespoon olive oil - $0.10
- Salt and pepper to taste - $0.05

Instructions:

1. **Marinate Chicken:** In a bowl, combine chicken with harissa, olive oil, salt, and pepper. Let marinate for at least 15 minutes.
2. **Cook Chicken:** Heat a skillet over medium-high heat. Cook chicken for 7-10 minutes on each side until cooked through.
3. **Serve:** Serve with rice or couscous.

Total Cost: ~$2.65

Bunny Chow (South African)

Ingredients:

- 1 loaf white bread (for serving) - $1.00
- 1 can curry chickpeas (15 oz) - $0.80
- 1 onion, diced - $0.30
- 1 tablespoon curry powder - $0.10
- 1 tablespoon vegetable oil - $0.10
- Add 1/2 cup coconut milk - $0.50

Instructions:

1. **Sauté Onions:** Heat oil in a pot. Add diced onions and cook until soft (about 5 minutes).
2. **Add Chickpeas:** Stir in curry powder, add coconut milk and chickpeas. Simmer for 10 minutes.
3. **Prepare Bread:** Hollow out a piece of bread to make a bowl. Fill with chickpea curry.
4. **Serve:** Enjoy with the bread on the side.

Total Cost: ~$2.80

Somali Rice (Bariis Iskukaris)

Ingredients:

- 2 cups rice - $0.50
- 1 onion, chopped - $0.30
- 1 carrot, grated - $0.25
- 2 cups water - $0.00
- 1 tablespoon vegetable oil - $0.10
- Salt and spices to taste - $0.05
- Add 2 Tablespoon shredded carrots very fine - $0.18
- Add 1 teaspoon minced red onion - $0.22

Instructions:

1. **Sauté Onions:** Heat oil in a pot and sauté onions until soft (about 5 minutes).
2. **Add Rice and Water:** Stir in rice, grated carrot, and water. Bring to a boil, then cover and simmer on low heat for about 20 minutes until rice is cooked.
3. **Season and Serve:** Fluff the rice with a fork and season to taste. Serve with stewed meat or vegetables.

Total Cost: ~$1.60

Algerian Couscous with Vegetables

Ingredients:

- 1 cup couscous - $0.75
- 1 cup mixed frozen vegetables - $0.80
- 1 tablespoon olive oil - $0.10
- 1 cup water - $0.00
- Salt and pepper to taste - $0.05
- Add 1/4 diced cooked chicken $1.00

Instructions:

1. **Prepare Couscous:** In a pot, bring water to a boil and add salt. Stir in couscous, remove from heat, and cover for 5 minutes.
2. **Cook Vegetables:** In a skillet, heat olive oil. Add frozen vegetables, sautéing until heated through (about 5-7 minutes).
3. **Combine:** Fluff the couscous with a fork and mix in sautéed vegetables and add diced cooked chicken. Season with salt and pepper.
4. **Serve:** Enjoy as a light main dish or side.

Total Cost: ~$2.70

Mandarin Orange Chicken

Ingredients:

- 1/2 lb chicken thighs ($1.00)
- 1/2 cup canned mandarin oranges ($0.50)
- 1 tbsp soy sauce ($0.05)
- 1 tsp cornstarch ($0.05)
- 1 tbsp vegetable oil ($0.10)
- 1 cup cooked rice ($0.30)

Instructions:

1. **Prepare Chicken:** Cut chicken thighs into bite-sized pieces.
2. **Cook Chicken:** Heat vegetable oil in a skillet over medium heat. Add chicken and cook until browned and cooked through (about 5-7 minutes).
3. **Make Sauce:** In a small bowl, mix soy sauce and cornstarch with 1 tbsp of mandarin orange juice. Add the oranges to the skillet with the chicken.
4. **Combine:** Pour the sauce over the chicken and cook for 2-3 minutes until thickened. Serve over rice.

Total Cost: ~$3.00

Chicken Tikka Masala

Ingredients:

- 1/2 lb chicken thighs ($1.00)
- 1/2 cup canned tomato sauce ($0.40)
- 1/4 cup plain yogurt ($0.30)
- 1 tsp garam masala ($0.15)
- 1 tbsp vegetable oil ($0.10)
- 1 cup cooked rice ($0.30)

Instructions:

1. **Prepare Chicken:** Cut chicken into cubes and marinate in yogurt and garam masala for at least 15 minutes.
2. **Cook Chicken:** Heat oil in a pan over medium heat. Add chicken and cook for 5-7 minutes. Remove and set aside.
3. **Make Sauce:** In the same pan, add tomato sauce and simmer for 5 minutes. Add chicken back and cook for another 5 minutes.
4. **Serve:** Serve with cooked rice.

Total Cost: ~$2.95

Spaghetti Cacio e Pepe

Ingredients:

- 6 oz spaghetti ($0.60)
- 1/4 cup grated Parmesan cheese ($0.50)
- 1 tsp black pepper ($0.05)
- 1 tbsp olive oil ($0.10)

Instructions:

1. **Cook Spaghetti:** Boil water and cook spaghetti until al dente. Reserve 1/4 cup of pasta water before draining.
2. **Make Sauce:** Heat olive oil in a pan and toast black pepper for 30 seconds.
3. **Combine:** Add cooked spaghetti and reserved pasta water to the pan. Stir in Parmesan cheese until creamy. Serve immediately.

Total Cost: ~$1.25

Gnocchi al Gorgonzola

Ingredients:

- 1/2 lb gnocchi ($0.75)
- 1/4 cup gorgonzola cheese ($0.75)
- 1/4 cup heavy cream ($0.75)

Instructions:

1. **Cook Gnocchi:** Boil water, add gnocchi, and cook until they float (about 2-3 minutes). Drain.
2. **Make Sauce:** Melt gorgonzola cheese into it and add heavy cream.
3. **Combine:** Add cooked gnocchi and stir to coat with the sauce. Serve immediately.

Total Cost: ~$2.25

Mac 'n Cheese

Ingredients:

- 1 cup elbow macaroni ($0.40)
- 1/2 cup shredded cheese ($0.50)
- 1/4 cup heavy cream ($0.75)
- 1 tbsp butter ($0.10)
- Salt and pepper to taste ($0.05)

Instructions:

1. **Cook Pasta:** Boil water and cook macaroni. Drain.
2. **Make Sauce:** In the same pot, melt butter and add heavy cream. Add shredded cheese and stir until melted and creamy.
3. **Combine:** Stir in cooked macaroni and season with salt and pepper.

Total Cost: ~$1.15

Vegetable Fried Rice

Ingredients:

- 2 cups cooked rice ($0.30)
- 1/2 cup frozen mixed vegetables ($0.40)
- 1 egg ($0.15)
- 1 tbsp soy sauce ($0.05)
- 1 tbsp vegetable oil ($0.10)
- Add 1/4 cup diced cooked chicken ($1.00)

Instructions:

1. **Scramble Egg:** Heat oil in a skillet and scramble the egg. Remove from skillet.
2. **Fry Vegetables:** In the same skillet, cook vegetables until heated through.
3. **Combine:** Add rice, scrambled egg, diced cooked chicken and soy sauce. Stir-fry for 3-4 minutes. Serve immediately.

Total Cost: ~$1.00

Mini Chicken Tacos

Ingredients:

- 1/2 lb chicken thighs ($1.00)
- 4 small corn tortillas ($0.40)
- 1/4 cup salsa ($0.40)
- 1/4 cup shredded lettuce ($0.15)
- 1/4 cup shredded cheese ($0.20)
- Add 1/4 avocado diced ($0.55)
- Add 1 sprig of scallion diced ($0.22)

Instructions:

1. **Cook Chicken:** Cut chicken into small pieces and cook in a skillet until browned and cooked through.
2. **Warm Tortillas:** Heat tortillas for 30 seconds on each side.
3. **Assemble Tacos:** Fill each tortilla with chicken, salsa, lettuce, and cheese.

Total Cost: ~$2.15

Chicken Burrito Bowl

Ingredients:

- 1/2 lb chicken thighs ($1.00)
- 1 cup cooked rice ($0.30)
- 1/2 cup black beans ($0.30)
- 1/4 cup salsa ($0.40)

Instructions:

1. **Cook Chicken:** Cook the chicken until browned and fully cooked, then cut into small pieces.
2. **Warm Beans:** Heat the black beans in a pan until warmed through.
3. **Assemble Bowl:** Layer cooked rice, beans, chicken, and salsa in bowls. Serve warm.

Total Cost: ~$2.00

Sriracha Shrimp Bowl

Ingredients:

- 1/4 lb shrimp ($1.00)
- 1 cup cooked rice ($0.30)
- 1 tbsp Sriracha ($0.10)
- 1/2 cup frozen vegetables ($0.40)

Instructions:

1. **Cook Shrimp:** In a skillet, cook shrimp until pink and fully cooked. Add Sriracha and stir.
2. **Cook Vegetables:** In the same pan, cook frozen vegetables until heated.
3. **Assemble Bowl:** In bowls, layer rice, shrimp, and vegetables.

Total Cost: ~$1.80

Thai Red Curry with Chicken

Ingredients:

- 1/2 lb chicken thighs ($1.00)
- 1/2 cup canned coconut milk ($0.40)
- 1 tbsp red curry paste ($0.30)
- 1/2 cup frozen vegetables ($0.40)

Instructions:

1. **Cook Chicken:** Cut chicken into pieces and cook until browned.
2. **Make Curry:** Add red curry paste to the pan and cook for 1 minute. Stir in coconut milk.
3. **Add Vegetables:** Stir in the frozen vegetables and cook for 5 minutes. Serve over rice if desired.

Total Cost: ~$2.10

Beef Enchiladas

Ingredients:

- 1/4 lb ground beef ($1.00)
- 4 small corn tortillas ($0.40)
- 1/2 cup enchilada sauce ($0.50)
- 1/4 cup shredded cheese ($0.50)
- 1/4 cup canned black beans ($0.30)

Instructions:

1. **Cook Beef:** Brown ground beef in a skillet over medium heat and season with salt and pepper. Drain any excess fat.
2. **Assemble Enchiladas:** Fill each tortilla with a spoonful of beef, beans, and a bit of cheese. Roll them up and place them seam-side down in a baking dish.
3. **Bake:** Pour enchilada sauce over the tortillas and sprinkle with remaining cheese. Bake at 350°F for 15 minutes until cheese is melted and bubbly. Serve warm.

Total Cost: ~$2.70

Chicken Burrito Bowl

Ingredients:

- 1/2 lb chicken thighs ($1.00)
- 1 cup cooked rice ($0.30)
- 1/2 cup black beans ($0.30)
- 1/4 cup salsa ($0.40)
- 1/4 cup shredded lettuce ($0.20)

Instructions:

1. **Cook Chicken:** Cut chicken into small pieces and cook in a skillet until browned and fully cooked.
2. **Warm Beans:** Heat black beans in a pan until warmed through.
3. **Assemble Bowl:** In bowls, layer cooked rice, chicken, black beans, salsa, and lettuce.

Total Cost: ~$2.20

Vegetable Fried Rice

Ingredients:

- 2 cups cooked rice ($0.30)
- 1/2 cup frozen mixed vegetables ($0.40)
- 1 egg ($0.15)
- 1 tbsp soy sauce ($0.05)
- 1 tbsp vegetable oil ($0.10)

Instructions:

1. **Scramble Egg:** Heat oil in a skillet and scramble the egg. Remove from skillet.
2. **Fry Vegetables:** In the same skillet, cook vegetables until heated through.
3. **Combine:** Add rice, scrambled egg, and soy sauce. Stir-fry for 3-4 minutes. Serve warm.

Total Cost: ~$1.00

Teriyaki Chicken

Ingredients:

- 1/2 lb chicken thighs ($1.00)
- 2 tbsp teriyaki sauce ($0.20)
- 1/2 cup frozen vegetables ($0.40)
- 1 cup cooked rice ($0.30)
- 1 tbsp vegetable oil ($0.10)

Instructions:

1. **Cook Chicken:** Cut chicken into bite-sized pieces and cook in a skillet with vegetable oil until browned and fully cooked.
2. **Add Sauce:** Add teriyaki sauce to the pan and stir to coat the chicken.
3. **Cook Vegetables:** In the same skillet, add frozen vegetables and stir-fry until heated through. Serve with rice.

Total Cost: ~$2.00

Pasta Primavera

Ingredients:

- 6 oz pasta ($0.60)
- 1/2 cup mixed frozen vegetables ($0.40)
- 1/4 cup grated Parmesan cheese ($0.50)
- 1 tbsp olive oil ($0.10)
- Salt and pepper to taste ($0.05)

Instructions:

1. **Cook Pasta:** Boil water and cook pasta until al dente. Drain.
2. **Cook Vegetables:** In a skillet, heat olive oil and cook vegetables until heated through.
3. **Combine:** Add pasta to the skillet with vegetables. Stir in Parmesan cheese, salt, and pepper. Serve warm.

Total Cost: ~$1.65

Mushroom Risotto

Ingredients:

- 1/2 cup Arborio rice ($0.50)
- 1/2 cup mushrooms ($0.80)
- 1/4 cup Parmesan cheese ($0.50)
- 1 tbsp olive oil ($0.10)
- 1 cup vegetable broth ($0.20)

Instructions:

1. **Cook Mushrooms:** Heat olive oil in a pan and sauté mushrooms until softened.
2. **Cook Rice:** Add Arborio rice to the pan and toast for 1 minute. Gradually add vegetable broth, stirring constantly until rice is creamy and cooked through (about 15-20 minutes).
3. **Add Cheese:** Stir in Parmesan cheese and serve immediately.

Total Cost: ~$2.10

Baked Ziti

Ingredients:

- 6 oz ziti pasta ($0.60)
- 1/2 cup marinara sauce ($0.50)
- 1/4 cup shredded mozzarella cheese ($0.50)
- 1/4 cup ricotta cheese ($0.50)
- 1 tbsp olive oil ($0.10)

Instructions:

1. **Cook Pasta:** Boil water and cook ziti until al dente. Drain.
2. **Assemble:** Mix cooked ziti with marinara sauce and ricotta cheese. Pour into a baking dish, top with mozzarella, and drizzle with olive oil.
3. **Bake:** Bake at 350°F for 15 minutes until cheese is bubbly and melted. Serve warm.

Total Cost: ~$2.20

Chicken and Vegetable Wontons

Ingredients:

- 1/2 lb ground chicken ($1.00)
- 1/2 cup mixed frozen vegetables ($0.40)
- 10 wonton wrappers ($0.50)
- 1 tbsp soy sauce ($0.05)
- 1 tbsp vegetable oil ($0.10)
- Add 1 Tablespoon Chinese 5 spice ($0.10)
- Add salt and pepper to taste ($0.10)

Instructions:

1. **Prepare Filling:** Mix ground chicken, vegetables, 1 Tablespoon Chinese 5 spice, salt and pepper to taste and soy sauce in a bowl.
2. **Fill Wontons:** Place a spoonful of the mixture in the center of each wonton wrapper. Fold and seal the edges with water.
3. **Cook:** Heat vegetable oil in a skillet and pan-fry the wontons until golden and crispy on both sides. Serve warm.

Total Cost: ~$2.25

Shrimp Tacos

Ingredients:

- 1/4 lb shrimp ($1.00)
- 4 small corn tortillas ($0.40)
- 1/4 cup shredded lettuce ($0.15)
- 1/4 cup salsa ($0.40)
- 1 tbsp vegetable oil ($0.10)

Instructions:

1. **Cook Shrimp:** In a skillet, cook shrimp with oil until pink and fully cooked (about 3-4 minutes).
2. **Warm Tortillas:** Heat tortillas in a pan for 30 seconds on each side.
3. **Assemble Tacos:** Fill each tortilla with shrimp, lettuce, and salsa. Serve warm.

Total Cost: ~$2.05

Cauliflower Gnocchi

Ingredients:

- 1/2 lb cauliflower gnocchi ($1.50)
- 1/4 cup marinara sauce ($0.25)
- 1/4 cup Parmesan cheese ($0.50)
- 1 tbsp olive oil ($0.10)

Instructions:

1. **Cook Gnocchi:** Heat olive oil in a skillet and cook cauliflower gnocchi until golden and crispy (about 5-7 minutes).
2. **Add Sauce:** Add marinara sauce and cook for another 2 minutes until heated through.
3. **Serve:** Serve with grated Parmesan cheese on top.

Total Cost: ~$2.35

Moroccan Style Chicken

Ingredients:

- 1/2 lb chicken thighs ($1.00)
- 1/2 cup canned tomatoes ($0.30)
- 1/4 cup canned chickpeas ($0.30)
- 1 tsp ground cumin ($0.05)
- 1 tsp ground cinnamon ($0.05)
- 1 tbsp olive oil ($0.10)
- 1 cup cooked couscous ($0.40)
- Add salt and pepper to taste ($0.10)

Instructions:

1. **Cook Chicken:** Heat olive oil in a pan, season chicken with cumin and cinnamon, add salt and pepper to taste and cook until browned and fully cooked.
2. **Add Tomatoes & Chickpeas:** Stir in canned tomatoes and chickpeas. Simmer for 5-7 minutes.
3. **Serve:** Serve over cooked couscous.

Total Cost: ~$2.30

Vegetable Samosas

Ingredients:

- 1 potato, diced ($0.50)
- 1/2 cup frozen peas ($0.30)
- 1/2 onion, chopped ($0.20)
- 1 tsp curry powder ($0.10)
- 6 small wonton wrappers ($0.30)
- 1 tbsp vegetable oil ($0.10)
- Add salt and pepper to taste ($0.10)

Instructions:

1. **Cook Filling:** Boil diced potato until tender. Drain and mash. Cook onion and peas in a pan with curry powder and add salt and pepper to taste.
2. **Assemble Samosas:** Place a spoonful of the filling in each wonton wrapper and fold into triangles.
3. **Cook:** Pan-fry the samosas in oil until golden brown and crispy. Serve warm.

Total Cost: ~$1.60

Chicken Curry

Ingredients:

- 1/2 lb chicken thighs ($1.00)
- 1/2 cup canned coconut milk ($0.40)
- 1 tbsp curry powder ($0.10)
- 1/2 cup frozen vegetables ($0.40)
- 1 cup cooked rice ($0.30)
- Add salt and pepper to taste ($0.10)

Instructions:

1. **Cook Chicken:** Cut chicken into pieces and cook in a skillet until browned.
2. **Make Curry:** Add curry powder, coconut milk, salt and pepper to taste and frozen vegetables. Simmer for 5-7 minutes.
3. **Serve:** Serve with cooked rice.

Total Cost: ~$2.30

Shrimp Fried Rice

Ingredients:

- 1/4 lb shrimp ($1.00)
- 2 cups cooked rice ($0.30)
- 1/2 cup frozen peas and carrots ($0.40)
- 1 egg ($0.15)
- 1 tbsp soy sauce ($0.05)
- 1 tbsp vegetable oil ($0.10)
- Add salt and pepper to taste ($0.10)

Instructions:

1. **Cook Shrimp:** Heat oil in a pan and cook shrimp until pink. Remove and set aside.
2. **Fry Rice:** In the same pan, scramble the egg. Add cooked rice, vegetables, salt and pepper to taste and soy sauce. Stir-fry for 3-4 minutes.
3. **Combine:** Add shrimp back into the pan. Serve warm.

Total Cost: ~$2.10

Thai Green Curry

Ingredients:

- 1/2 lb chicken thighs ($1.00)
- 1/2 cup canned coconut milk ($0.40)
- 1 tbsp green curry paste ($0.30)
- 1/2 cup frozen vegetables ($0.40)
- 1 cup cooked rice ($0.30)
- Add salt and pepper to taste ($0.10)

Instructions:

1. **Cook Chicken:** Cut chicken into pieces and cook in a skillet until browned.
2. **Make Curry:** Stir in green curry paste, coconut milk, salt and pepper to taste and vegetables. Simmer for 5-7 minutes.
3. **Serve:** Serve with cooked rice.

Total Cost: ~$2.50

Indian Style Masoor Dal

Ingredients:

- 1/2 cup red lentils ($0.40)
- 1/2 onion, chopped ($0.20)
- 1 tsp cumin seeds ($0.05)
- 1/2 tsp turmeric ($0.05)
- 1 clove garlic, minced ($0.05)
- 1 tbsp vegetable oil ($0.10)
- 1 cup cooked rice ($0.30)
- Add salt and pepper to taste ($0.10)

Instructions:

1. **Cook Lentils:** Boil lentils in water with turmeric until soft.
2. **Make Tadka:** In a separate pan, heat oil, add cumin seeds, onion, salt and pepper to taste and garlic. Fry until golden.
3. **Combine:** Mix the lentils with the tadka and serve with cooked rice.

Total Cost: ~$1.25

BBQ Chicken Teriyaki

Ingredients:

- 1/2 lb chicken thighs ($1.00)
- 2 tbsp teriyaki sauce ($0.20)
- 1/4 cup BBQ sauce ($0.30)
- 1/2 cup frozen vegetables ($0.40)
- 1 cup cooked rice ($0.30)
- Add salt and pepper to taste ($0.10)

Instructions:

1. **Cook Chicken:** Grill or pan-fry chicken until fully cooked.
2. **Add Sauces:** Combine BBQ sauce and teriyaki sauce, salt and pepper to taste and coat the cooked chicken.
3. **Serve:** Serve with frozen vegetables and rice.

Total Cost: ~$2.30

Chicken Pot Pie

Ingredients:

- 1/2 lb chicken thighs ($1.00)
- 1/2 cup mixed frozen vegetables ($0.40)
- 1/4 cup heavy cream ($0.24)
- 1 tbsp flour ($0.05)
- 1 tbsp butter ($0.10)
- 1 small pie crust ($0.50)
- Add salt and pepper to taste ($0.10)

Instructions:

1. **Cook Chicken:** Dice chicken and cook in a pan until browned.
2. **Make Filling:** Stir in butter, flour, and heavy cream to create a creamy sauce. Add frozen vegetables, salt and pepper to taste and cooked chicken.
3. **Assemble & Bake:** Pour the filling into a pie dish, cover with pie crust, and bake at 350°F for 20 minutes until golden brown.

Total Cost: ~$2.39

Vegetable Masala Burgers

Ingredients:

- 1/2 cup chickpeas ($0.30)
- 1/2 potato, mashed ($0.25)
- 1/2 onion, chopped ($0.20)
- 1 tsp garam masala ($0.10)
- 1 tbsp vegetable oil ($0.10)
- 2 burger buns ($0.60)
- Add salt and pepper to taste ($0.10)

1. **Make Patties:** Mix chickpeas, mashed potato, onion, salt and pepper to taste and garam masala. Form into patties.
2. **Cook Patties:** Heat oil in a pan and cook the patties until golden brown on both sides.
3. **Assemble:** Serve the patties on burger buns.

Total Cost: ~$1.65

Cheese Pizza with a Cauliflower Crust

Ingredients:

- 1/2 head cauliflower ($1.00)
- 1/2 cup shredded mozzarella cheese ($0.50)
- 1/4 cup pizza sauce ($0.30)
- 1 egg ($0.15)
- 1 tsp Italian seasoning ($0.05)
- Add salt and pepper to taste ($0.10)

Instructions:

1. **Make Crust:** Grate the cauliflower and steam it for 5 minutes. Squeeze out excess water and mix with egg, half of the mozzarella, salt and pepper to taste and Italian seasoning.
2. **Bake Crust:** Press the mixture into a pizza shape on a baking sheet and bake at 400ºF for 15 minutes until firm.
3. **Top & Bake:** Spread pizza sauce over the crust, add remaining mozzarella, and bake for another 5 minutes until cheese is melted.

Total Cost: ~$2.20

Chicken Cilantro Mini Wontons

Ingredients:

- 1/2 lb ground chicken ($1.00)
- 1 tbsp fresh cilantro, chopped ($0.10)
- 1 clove garlic, minced ($0.05)
- 10 wonton wrappers ($0.50)
- 1 tbsp soy sauce ($0.05)
- Add salt and pepper to taste ($0.10)

Instructions:

1. **Prepare Filling:** Mix ground chicken with cilantro, garlic, salt and pepper to taste and soy sauce.
2. **Assemble Wontons:** Place a spoonful of filling into each wonton wrapper and fold into triangles.
3. **Cook Wontons:** Pan-fry the wontons in oil until golden and crispy. Serve warm.

Total Cost: ~$1.80

Mac and Cheese Bites

Ingredients:

- 1 cup cooked macaroni ($0.30)
- 1/4 cup shredded cheddar cheese ($0.50)
- 1/4 cup milk ($0.10)
- 1 tbsp butter ($0.10)
- 1 egg ($0.15)
- 1/4 cup breadcrumbs ($0.20)

Instructions:

1. **Make Mac & Cheese:** Melt butter in a pan, add milk, and stir in shredded cheddar until melted. Mix with cooked macaroni.
2. **Form Bites:** Once cooled, stir in an egg and form the mixture into small bite-sized balls. Roll in breadcrumbs.
3. **Bake:** Place on a baking sheet and bake at 375ºF for 10-12 minutes until crispy.

Total Cost: ~$2.35

Fish Sticks

Ingredients:

- 1/4 lb white fish fillets ($1.00)
- 1/4 cup breadcrumbs ($0.20)
- 1 egg ($0.15)
- 1 tbsp vegetable oil ($0.10)
- Salt and pepper to taste ($0.05)

Instructions:

1. **Prepare Fish:** Cut fish fillets into strips and season with salt and pepper.
2. **Coat Fish:** Dip fish strips into a beaten egg, then coat with breadcrumbs.
3. **Cook:** Heat oil in a skillet and fry fish sticks until golden brown on both sides. Serve warm.

Total Cost: ~$1.50

Hatch Chile Mac & Cheese

Ingredients:

- 1 cup cooked macaroni ($0.30)
- 1/4 cup shredded cheddar cheese ($0.50)
- 1/4 cup heavy cream ($0.23)
- 1 tbsp butter ($0.10)
- 2 tbsp chopped Hatch chiles (canned or fresh) ($0.40)

Instructions:

1. **Make Mac & Cheese:** Melt butter in a pan, add heavy cream, and stir in shredded cheddar until melted. Mix with cooked macaroni.
2. **Add Chiles:** Stir in chopped Hatch chiles and cook for an additional 2-3 minutes.
3. **Serve:** Serve warm with extra cheese on top if desired.

Total Cost: ~$1.53

Kung Pao Chicken

Ingredients:

- 1/2 lb chicken thighs ($1.00)
- 1/4 cup peanuts ($0.30)
- 1/2 cup bell peppers, chopped ($0.40)
- 1 tbsp soy sauce ($0.05)
- 1 tbsp hoisin sauce ($0.20)
- 1 tbsp vegetable oil ($0.10)
- 1 cup cooked rice ($0.30)
- Add salt and pepper to taste ($0.10)

Instructions:

1. **Cook Chicken:** Cut chicken into bite-sized pieces, add salt and pepper to taste and cook in a skillet with vegetable oil until browned.
2. **Add Vegetables & Sauce:** Add bell peppers, peanuts, soy sauce, and hoisin sauce. Cook for an additional 5-7 minutes.
3. **Serve:** Serve with cooked rice.

Total Cost: ~$2.45

Chicken Burritos

Ingredients:

- 1/2 lb chicken thighs ($1.00)
- 1/2 cup cooked rice ($0.30)
- 1/4 cup canned black beans ($0.20)
- 2 large tortillas ($0.40)
- 1/4 cup salsa ($0.30)
- Add salt and pepper to taste ($0.10)

Instructions:

1. **Cook Chicken:** Cut chicken into small pieces and add salt and pepper to taste and cook in a skillet until browned.
2. **Assemble Burritos:** Place rice, black beans, cooked chicken, and salsa into each tortilla. Roll up tightly.
3. **Serve:** Serve warm, or pan-fry for a crispy exterior.

Total Cost: ~$2.20

Mahi Mahi Burgers

Ingredients:

- 1/4 lb mahi mahi fillets ($1.00)
- 2 burger buns ($0.60)
- 1 tbsp mayonnaise ($0.10)
- 1/4 cup lettuce ($0.20)
- 1/4 tsp lemon juice ($0.05)
- 1 tbsp vegetable oil ($0.10)
- Add salt and pepper to taste ($0.10)

Instructions:

1. **Cook Fish:** Season the mahi mahi with salt, pepper, and lemon juice, then pan-fry in oil until cooked through.
2. **Assemble Burgers:** Spread mayonnaise on the buns, add lettuce, and place the cooked mahi mahi on top.
3. **Serve:** Serve warm with extra lemon juice if desired.

Total Cost: ~$2.15

Sublime Ice Cream Sandwiches

Ingredients:

- 4 chocolate chip cookies ($0.60)
- 1/2 cup vanilla ice cream ($0.60)

Instructions:

1. **Assemble Sandwiches:** Scoop ice cream onto two cookies, and place another cookie on top to form a sandwich.
2. **Freeze:** Place the sandwiches in the freezer for 30 minutes to firm up.
3. **Serve:** Serve cold and enjoy!

Total Cost: ~$1.20

Mochi Ice Cream (Various Flavors)

Ingredients:

- 1/2 cup ice cream (any flavor) ($0.60)
- 1/4 cup sweet rice flour (Mochiko) ($0.50)
- 1 tbsp sugar ($0.05)
- 1/4 cup water ($0.00)
- Cornstarch for dusting ($0.10)

Instructions:

1. **Make Dough:** Mix sweet rice flour, sugar, and water. Microwave for 1 minute, stir, and microwave for 30 more seconds.
2. **Shape Mochi:** Dust a surface with cornstarch, roll out the dough, and cut into small circles.
3. **Assemble Mochi:** Wrap each ice cream ball in the dough, then freeze for 1 hour before serving.

Total Cost: ~$1.25

Hold the Cone! Mini Ice Cream Cones

Ingredients:

- 4 mini sugar cones ($0.50)
- 1/2 cup vanilla ice cream ($0.60)
- 1/4 cup melted chocolate chips ($0.40)

Instructions:

1. **Fill Cones:** Scoop ice cream into each mini cone.
2. **Dip in Chocolate:** Dip the top of each cone in melted chocolate.
3. **Freeze & Serve:** Freeze cones for 15 minutes, then serve.

Total Cost: ~$1.50

Chocolate Lava Cakes

Ingredients:

- 1/4 cup chocolate chips ($0.40)
- 2 tbsp butter ($0.20)
- 1 egg ($0.15)
- 1 tbsp sugar ($0.05)
- 1 tbsp flour ($0.05)

Instructions:

1. **Make Batter:** Melt chocolate and butter together, then whisk in egg, sugar, and flour.
2. **Bake:** Pour into two greased ramekins and bake at 425°F for 10-12 minutes.
3. **Serve:** Let cool for a minute, then serve with a spoon to reveal the molten center.

Total Cost: ~$0.85

Vanilla Ice Cream Bon Bons

Ingredients:

- 1/2 cup vanilla ice cream ($0.60)
- 1/4 cup melted chocolate chips ($0.40)

Instructions:

1. **Scoop Ice Cream:** Form small balls of ice cream and freeze for 10 minutes.
2. **Coat in Chocolate:** Dip each ice cream ball in melted chocolate and place on parchment paper.
3. **Freeze & Serve:** Freeze for 1 hour and serve cold.

Total Cost: ~$1.00

Mini Cheesecake Cones

Ingredients:

- 2 sugar cones ($0.30)
- 1/4 cup cream cheese ($0.40)
- 1 tbsp sugar ($0.05)
- 1/4 cup crushed graham crackers ($0.20)

Instructions:

1. **Make Filling:** Mix cream cheese and sugar until smooth.
2. **Assemble Cones:** Fill sugar cones with the cream cheese mixture and sprinkle crushed graham crackers on top.
3. **Serve:** Chill for 10 minutes before serving.

Total Cost: ~$0.95

Gone Bananas! (Frozen Chocolate-Covered Banana Slices)

Ingredients:

- 1 banana, sliced ($0.30)
- 1/4 cup melted chocolate chips ($0.40)
- Add wooden skewer (4) ($0.33)

Instructions:

1. **Prepare Bananas:** Slice banana into rounds.
2. **Dip in Chocolate:** Dip each banana slice into the melted chocolate and place on parchment paper and place wooden skewers in center.
3. **Freeze & Serve:** Freeze for 1 hour before serving.

Total Cost: ~$1.03

Danish Kringle (Frozen Pastry)

Ingredients:

- 1/2 sheet puff pastry ($1.00)
- 1/4 cup almond paste ($0.50)
- 1 tbsp sugar ($0.05)
- 1 tbsp butter ($0.10)

Instructions:

1. **Prepare Pastry:** Roll out puff pastry and spread almond paste in the center.
2. **Shape & Bake:** Fold the pastry into a ring, sprinkle with sugar, and bake at 375°F for 15-20 minutes.
3. **Serve:** Let cool for a few minutes, then serve warm.

Total Cost: ~$1.65

Macarons (Assorted Flavors)

Ingredients:

- 1/4 cup almond flour ($0.70)
- 1/4 cup powdered sugar ($0.15)
- 1 egg white ($0.15)
- 1 tbsp sugar ($0.05)
- Food coloring (optional) ($0.10)

Instructions:

1. **Make Batter:** Beat egg white and sugar until stiff peaks form. Fold in almond flour and powdered sugar.
2. **Pipe & Bake:** Pipe small rounds onto a baking sheet and bake at 300°F for 12-15 minutes.
3. **Assemble:** Once cool, sandwich with your choice of filling.

Total Cost: ~$1.15

Chocolate-Covered Strawberries

Ingredients:

- 6 strawberries ($0.60)
- 1/4 cup melted chocolate chips ($0.40)

Instructions:

1. **Dip Strawberries:** Dip each strawberry into the melted chocolate and place on parchment paper.
2. **Chill & Serve:** Refrigerate for 15 minutes until the chocolate hardens, then serve.

Total Cost: ~$1.00

Peppermint Mini Ice Cream Cones

Ingredients:

- 4 mini sugar cones ($0.50)
- 1/2 cup peppermint ice cream ($0.80)

Instructions:

1. **Fill Cones:** Scoop peppermint ice cream into each mini cone.
2. **Freeze:** Place the cones in the freezer for 15 minutes to firm up.
3. **Serve:** Serve cold and enjoy the refreshing taste of peppermint!

Total Cost: ~$1.30

Organic Chocolate Chip Cookie Dough Bites

Ingredients:

- 1 cup organic flour ($0.40)
- 1/2 cup chocolate chips ($0.60)
- 1/2 cup butter, softened ($0.80)
- 1/4 cup brown sugar ($0.10)
- 1/4 cup granulated sugar ($0.05)

Instructions:

1. **Make Dough:** In a bowl, cream together the softened butter, brown sugar, and granulated sugar. Mix in flour and chocolate chips until well combined.
2. **Form Bites:** Roll into small balls and place on a plate.
3. **Chill & Serve:** Refrigerate for 30 minutes before serving.

Total Cost: ~$1.95

Brownie Crisp Coffee Ice Cream Sandwiches

Ingredients:

- 2 brownie squares ($0.60)
- 1/2 cup coffee ice cream ($0.80)

Instructions:

1. **Assemble Sandwiches:** Place a scoop of coffee ice cream between two brownie squares to form a sandwich.
2. **Freeze:** Place in the freezer for 30 minutes to firm up.
3. **Serve:** Enjoy your decadent brownie ice cream sandwich!

**Note- I have made my own brownie mixture and pout it in a waffle iron. You can do it that way as well

Total Cost: ~$1.40

Non-Dairy Oat Frozen Dessert Sandwiches

Ingredients:

- 4 oat cookies ($0.50)
- 1/2 cup non-dairy ice cream ($0.80)

Instructions:

1. **Assemble Sandwiches:** Scoop non-dairy ice cream between two oat cookies.
2. **Freeze:** Place the sandwiches in the freezer for 30 minutes.
3. **Serve:** Serve cold and enjoy!

Total Cost: ~$1.30

Mango & Sticky Rice Spring Rolls

Ingredients:

- 1 cup cooked sticky rice ($0.60)
- 1 ripe mango, sliced ($0.80)
- 6 Noris sheets ($0.50)
- Add salt and pepper to taste .10

Instructions:

1. **Assemble Rolls:** Place a spoonful of sticky rice and mango slices on each noris sheets and roll tightly.
2. **Serve Fresh:** Serve immediately or chill for 10 minutes in the refrigerator before serving.

Total Cost: ~$2.00

Mini Pumpkin Ginger Ice Cream Cones

Ingredients:

- 4 mini sugar cones ($0.50)
- 1/2 cup pumpkin ice cream ($0.80)

Instructions:

1. **Fill Cones:** Scoop pumpkin ice cream into each mini cone.
2. **Freeze:** Place in the freezer for 15 minutes to firm up.
3. **Serve:** Serve cold for a delightful fall treat!

Total Cost: ~$1.30

Chocolate French Toast Bites

Ingredients:

- 2 slices of bread ($0.40)
- 1 egg ($0.15)
- 1/4 cup milk ($0.10)
- 2 tbsp chocolate spread ($0.30)
- Powdered sugar for dusting ($0.05)

Instructions:

1. **Prepare Batter:** Whisk egg and milk together in a bowl.
2. **Coat Bread:** Dip bread slices into the egg mixture, then cook on a skillet until golden brown on both sides.
3. **Serve:** Spread chocolate on top, dust with powdered sugar, and cut into bite-sized pieces.

Total Cost: ~$1.30

Speculoos Cookie Butter Ice Cream Cups

Ingredients:

- 1/2 cup vanilla ice cream ($0.60)
- 2 tbsp speculoos cookie butter ($0.50)
- Crushed speculoos cookies for topping ($0.20)

Instructions:

1. **Prepare Cups:** Scoop vanilla ice cream into small cups.
2. **Layer:** Add a layer of speculoos cookie butter on top and sprinkle crushed cookies.
3. **Serve:** Enjoy your delicious and creamy dessert!

Total Cost: ~$1.30

Caramel Ginger Ice Cream Sundaes

Ingredients:

- 1/2 cup vanilla ice cream ($0.60)
- 2 tbsp caramel sauce ($0.40)
- 1 tbsp candied ginger, chopped ($0.50)

Instructions:

1. **Assemble Sundaes:** Scoop vanilla ice cream into bowls.
2. **Top & Serve:** Drizzle with caramel sauce and sprinkle with chopped candied ginger.

Total Cost: ~$1.50

Chocolate Brooklyn Babka Slices

Ingredients:

- 2 slices chocolate babka ($1.00)
- 1 tbsp butter ($0.10)

Instructions:

1. **Toast Babka:** Spread butter on each slice and toast until warm.
2. **Serve:** Serve warm, optionally with a scoop of ice cream.

Total Cost: ~$1.10

Strawberry Oat Frozen Delight

Ingredients:

- 1 cup frozen strawberries ($0.80)
- 1/2 cup non-dairy oat milk ($0.60)
- 1/4 cup maple syrup ($0.40)

Instructions:

1. **Blend Ingredients:** Combine frozen strawberries, oat milk, and maple syrup in a blender. Blend until smooth.
2. **Freeze Mixture:** Pour the mixture into a container and freeze for at least 2 hours.
3. **Serve:** Scoop out and serve as a refreshing frozen dessert.

Total Cost: ~$1.80

Chocolate Mini Cones Without Dairy

Ingredients:

- 4 mini sugar cones ($0.50)
- 1/2 cup dairy-free chocolate ice cream ($0.80)

Instructions:

1. **Fill Cones:** Scoop dairy-free chocolate ice cream into each mini cone.
2. **Freeze:** Place the cones in the freezer for 15 minutes to set.
3. **Serve:** Enjoy your rich chocolate treat!

Total Cost: ~$1.30

Berry Bliss Chocolate-Covered Strawberries

Ingredients:

- 6 strawberries ($0.60)
- 1/4 cup melted dark chocolate chips ($0.40)

Instructions:

1. **Dip Strawberries:** Dip each strawberry into the melted chocolate and place on parchment paper.
2. **Chill:** Refrigerate for 15 minutes to allow chocolate to harden.
3. **Serve:** Enjoy your decadent chocolate-covered strawberries!

Total Cost: ~$1.00

Apple Blossom Treats

Ingredients:

- 2 apples, sliced ($1.00)
- 1 tbsp cinnamon ($0.05)
- 1 tbsp sugar ($0.05)
- 1 sheet of puff pastry ($0.90)

Instructions:

1. **Prepare Filling:** Mix sliced apples with cinnamon and sugar.
2. **Assemble Blossoms:** Roll out puff pastry, cut into squares, and place apple mixture in the center. Fold corners to form a blossom shape.
3. **Bake & Serve:** Bake at 375°F for 20 minutes or until golden brown. Serve warm.

Total Cost: ~$2.00

Mini Key Lime Pie Cups

Ingredients:

- 1/2 cup Greek yogurt ($0.60)
- 1/4 cup key lime juice ($0.70)
- 1 tbsp sugar ($0.05)
- 4 graham cracker crumbs ($0.20)

Instructions:

1. **Mix Filling:** In a bowl, mix yogurt, key lime juice, and sugar until smooth.
2. **Assemble Cups:** Divide the mixture into small cups and sprinkle graham cracker crumbs on top.
3. **Chill & Serve:** Chill in the refrigerator for 30 minutes before serving.

Total Cost: ~$1.55

Cold Brew Latte Dessert Bars

Ingredients:

- 1/2 cup cold brew coffee ($0.40)
- 1/2 cup whipped cream ($0.80)
- 1/4 cup sugar ($0.05)
- 1/4 cup gelatin powder ($0.50)

Instructions:

1. **Dissolve Gelatin:** Mix gelatin with cold brew coffee and sugar until dissolved.
2. **Pour Mixture:** Pour the mixture into a small baking dish and refrigerate for 1-2 hours until set.
3. **Cut & Serve:** Cut into bars and serve chilled with whipped cream.

Total Cost: ~$1.75

Pumpkin Cheesecake Bites

Ingredients:

- 1/2 cup cream cheese ($0.80)
- 1/4 cup pumpkin puree ($0.30)
- 1/4 cup sugar ($0.05)
- 1 tsp pumpkin spice ($0.05)
- Add candy topping ($0.20)

Instructions:

1. **Mix Ingredients:** In a bowl, mix cream cheese, pumpkin puree, sugar, and pumpkin spice until smooth.
2. **Chill Mixture:** Pour into small cups and refrigerate for 1 hour.
3. **Serve:** Serve chilled as delightful pumpkin cheesecake bites.

Total Cost: ~$1.40

Matcha Green Tea Mochi Ice Cream

Ingredients:

- 1/2 cup vanilla ice cream ($0.60)
- 1/4 cup sweet rice flour (Mochiko) ($0.50)
- 1 tbsp sugar ($0.05)
- 1/4 cup water ($0.00)
- Matcha powder for dusting ($0.10)

Instructions:

1. **Make Dough:** Mix sweet rice flour, sugar, and water. Microwave for 1 minute, stir, and microwave for another 30 seconds.
2. **Shape Mochi:** Dust a surface with matcha powder, roll out the dough, and cut into small circles.
3. **Assemble Mochi:** Wrap each ice cream ball in the dough, then freeze for 1 hour before serving.

Total Cost: ~$1.25

Variety Pack Sweet Bites

Ingredients:

- 2 store-bought cookies ($0.50)
- 1 mini brownie ($0.40)
- 1 mini muffin ($0.60)
- Add cupcake cups ($0.15)

Instructions:

1. **Assemble Variety Pack:** Arrange cookies, brownie, and mini muffin on a plate.
2. **Serve:** Enjoy your assorted sweet bites together.

Total Cost: ~$1.65

Chocolate Lava Cake Delights

Ingredients:

- 1/4 cup chocolate chips ($0.40)
- 2 tbsp butter ($0.20)
- 1 egg ($0.15)
- 1 tbsp sugar ($0.05)
- 1 tbsp flour ($0.05)
- Add chocolate syrup ($0.45)

Instructions:

1. **Prepare Batter:** Melt chocolate and butter together. Whisk in egg, sugar, and flour until smooth.
2. **Bake:** Pour into two greased ramekins and bake at 425°F for 10-12 minutes.
3. **Serve:** Let cool briefly, then serve with a spoon to enjoy the molten center.

Total Cost: ~$1.30